D1605752

FACE-OFF AT THE SUMMIT

FACE-OFF AT THE SUMMIT

by Ken Dryden with Mark Mulvoy

A Sports Illustrated Book
Little, Brown & Company — Boston–Toronto

T 03/73

Library of Congress Cataloging in Publication Data

Dryden, Ken, 1947-
    Face-off at the summit.

    1. Hockey.   I. Mulvoy, Mark, joint author.
II. Title.
GV847.7.D79   796.9'62   73-3031
ISBN 0-316-19360-7

Sports Illustrated Books
are published by
Little, Brown and Company
in association with
Sports Illustrated Magazine

Published simultaneously in Canada
by Little, Brown & Company (Canada) Limited

For Lynda

I met Ken Dryden for the first time on a cold Tuesday night early in December of 1966 in Potsdam, New York. Dryden was a sophomore goaltender for Cornell University then, and I was doing a story on his coach, Ned Harkness, for *Sports Illustrated.* That night Cornell, with Dryden playing spectacularly in goal, upset Clarkson — rated the East's best college hockey team — in overtime. At the time, Dryden was totally bald on top, because his Cornell teammates had initiated him onto the varsity the night before with the ritualistic shave.

A few months later I saw Dryden after a game in Boston. He simply shook his head and smiled — or at least I think he smiled. As it had turned out, my story on Harkness had not been received very well in Ithaca, New York.

In January of 1968 I was having lunch with Sam Pollock, the shrewd general manager of the Montreal Canadiens, in his office at the Montreal Forum, and Pollock kept lamenting over his club's problems in goal.

"Sam," I said, "there's a big kid down at Cornell University named Dryden and he's —"

"Yes, I know all about him," Sam said, smiling. "We've got him on our negotiation list already."

So, three years later, in March of 1971, I ran into Dryden again, this time in the press box at the Forum a few days after the Canadiens had recalled him from their local farm team in the American Hockey League. We spent several hours during the game that night talking about college hockey, and the next night we had dinner at the Hot Stove Lounge in Maple Leaf Gardens in Toronto. "I don't know what I'm doing here," Dryden said during dinner. "I was playing well in the American League, now I'm here for the ride. They're not even dressing me."

Dryden, as it developed, was Montreal's secret weapon for the play-offs. The Canadiens played Dryden in only six games during the closing weeks of the National Hockey League season, then they tossed him against the record-setting Boston Bruins in the Stanley Cup play-offs. Backed by Dryden's brilliant goaltending, Montreal upset the Bruins in seven games, eliminated the Minnesota North Stars in six games, and then won the Stanley Cup by beating the Chicago Black Hawks in seven games. Dryden was named the Most Valuable Player of the play-offs.

Shortly afterwards, Dryden called me at home to say that he was going to work with Ralph Nader's Raiders in Washington, D.C., during the summer and he wondered if I knew where he could get an apartment. He eventually found a suburban apartment with the help of my sister, who knew of a place that some of her teacher friends were trying to sublease for the summer. Several times that summer Dryden called me at home to talk hockey. "I don't think the people down here know there's such a game," he complained. (Now Washington will have its own NHL franchise for the 1974–75 season.)

When I proposed the idea for this book to Dryden last August, he was completely in favor. He had been thinking about keeping a record of the daily events of the Team Canada–Soviet Union series for his own purposes, but he said the thought of putting his feelings and observations into a book also had great appeal.

"What I want," he said, "is an honest diary. I will not plug things into holes just so they will fit. What happens on a Tuesday will not be inserted into a spot on Friday just to make for good reading. As a result, there will be some contradictions in the book. Or apparent contradictions. What I feel one day, I may not feel the next. But I want the book to record not only my final feelings but also all the feelings that contributed to that end."

As Team Canada traveled through Canada, and then on to Sweden, Russia and Czechoslovakia, Dryden and I did not converse that much, since we both had our own work to do, his on the ice, mine for *Sports Illustrated*. Each day, Dryden gave me a progress report on his tapes, and we compared notes on where we had been. Dryden did not carry his tape recorder everywhere with him; instead, he wrote notes to himself on little scraps of paper and filed them in his pockets. Each night he sat down and relived his day for the tape recorder.

Once back home from Moscow, I spent several weeks breaking down the tapes and typing them double-spaced onto one hundred and sixty-five pages of 8 x 11 paper. All in all, Dryden's tapes totaled some eighty-five thousand words; in turn, I condensed them into the text you will read here.

Many words of thanks must go to my wife, Trish, who kept Kelly and Kris out of the den while I worked and kept plenty of tuna fish sandwiches in the refrigerator; to Charles Everitt, the editor who listened to my idea for the book and soon convinced Little, Brown that it would be a worthwhile project; to Sara Hill, a Boston Bruins fan who did the close checking, backchecking and forechecking on the manuscript; and to Managing Editor Andre Laguerre and Senior Editor Ken Rudeen of *Sports Illustrated*. The rest is Ken's story.

MARK MULVOY

Rye, New York
December 20, 1972

FACE-OFF AT THE SUMMIT

June 25

My wife Lynda and I were enjoying a leisurely brunch at a café in Vienna, Austria, around 1 P.M. According to my calculations, it was about 8 A.M. in Rochester, New York, so I went to place the collect call once again.

"Won't you wake someone up?" Lynda asked.

"Whoever it is probably is on the seventh green by now," I said.

It was Harry Sinden, and I did wake him up. The connection was terrible but I understood Harry perfectly. He was going to coach Team Canada in the series against the Soviet Union in September, and he wanted me to be one of his goaltenders.

It was not a tough decision. In fact, I could hardly say yes fast enough.

For one thing, playing the Russians in September certainly would be more fun than training camp with the Montreal Canadiens in Kentville, Nova Scotia, and the exhibition games when you have to skate around a couple of times each period to get the fog off the ice. For another, like about twenty-two million other Canadians, I wanted to play the Russians.

Harry told me the other goaltenders would be Gerry Cheevers of the Boston Bruins and Tony Esposito of the Chicago Black Hawks. He also mentioned the names of a few of the Montreal players who would be on the squad, like J. C. Tremblay, Yvan Cournoyer and the Mahovlich brothers, Frank and Peter.

I told Harry that I'd be back in Canada at the end of July to take some law exams at McGill University, and he said that training camp would begin in Toronto at Maple Leaf Gardens on Sunday, August 13.

Driving into Montreal from the airport at Dorval, Lynda and I noticed a sign on a billboard along the highway. TO RUSSIA WITH HULL. "Wonder what that means," I said to her. We learned exactly what it meant once we got back to our apartment, read the newspapers, and made some phone calls.

While we were vacationing in Europe there had been a tremendous hassle in Canada over the makeup of the team that would play against the Soviet Union. According to the text of the agreement made in April between the Canadians and the Russians, only National Hockey League players would be allowed to skate for Team Canada.

At the time, few people expected that many established players in the NHL would be jumping over to the fledgling World Hockey Association, so that clause seemed natural and insignificant. But then the new league began to throw around millions of dollars — like three million for Hull's signature and two and a half million for Sanderson's moustache — and suddenly hockey had its first money war.

So, when Sinden announced his original roster for the games, he included the names of Hull, Sanderson, Tremblay and Cheevers with asterisks after them. They had all jumped to the WHA, and according to the agreement, unless they signed NHL contracts before August 13, they would not be permitted to play against the Russians.

All over Canada irate citizens rebelled at the possible exclusion of the four WHA defectors from Team Canada. Telegrams with thousands of signatures were sent to newspapers and radio stations demanding that the four players be allowed to join the team. TO RUSSIA WITH HULL signs sprang up everywhere. Editorial writers from Halifax to Victoria blasted the NHL for its cavalier attitude, making note of the fact that fourteen of the sixteen NHL owners lived in the United States and cared little about a matter so fiercely important to more than twenty-two million patriotic Canadians.

Even the prime minister, Pierre Trudeau, got into the act and said that the four players definitely should be allowed to represent Canada against the Soviet Union.

It was a thorny problem but one that could easily have been rectified if all the involved parties had desired to do so. The NHL owners were very protective and defensive about their league and simply were not willing to lend any status whatsoever to the new league. By giving the WHA players permission to skate with Team Canada, the NHL would have provided the WHA with some instant prestige; but by refusing permission, it could be said that the NHL gave prestige to the WHA anyway. Also, the NHL owners probably felt they would weaken the legal actions pending against the defectors to the WHA by allowing them to play in the series.

Because the NHL remained adamant, there was a suggestion that Hull, Sanderson, Tremblay, Cheevers and the rest of us should band together and play the Russians independently, under the sponsorship of the NHL Players' Association. This possible solution presented two serious problems:

1) If a player became injured during the Canada-Russia series and was unable to play during the regular schedule, his NHL team would not have to honor any salary or contractual agreements it had made with him. But if Team Canada played as Team NHL, the NHL owners had agreed to consider all Team Canada exer-

[5]

cises as an extension of the normal training camp and therefore would guarantee full salary benefits in case of injury to any player. The cost for that insurance, by the way, is apparently about three hundred and fifty thousand dollars a year.

2) Quite understandably, many players did not want to get involved in the series without the good wishes of their owners, general managers and coaches. In other words, they did not want to risk making life miserable for themselves back home. Why alienate the people who are paying your salary?

So Hockey Canada had to make a decision. It could follow the NHL plan and exclude the four WHA players from Team Canada's roster; play the series without the cooperation of the NHL and lose a great majority of the NHL players as a result; or cancel the series entirely. The result: the four WHA players were left off the team.

Apparently, the decision was based on the fact that the series between Canada's pros and Russia's amateurs had been desired for a long, long time, and was now close to becoming a reality. No one wanted to make a move that would endanger it. When I first heard of the decision I was extremely upset, because I felt we should have the best possible team ready to play against the Russians, who would be sending their best players against us. Team Canada would not be Team Canada. It would be Team NHL and lack some of Canada's best players.

Obviously, the NHL felt that its chances of winning would not be hurt by the absence of Hull, Sanderson, Tremblay and Cheevers, all of whom, remember, played in the NHL the previous season and for years before that. I wonder what the NHL's reaction would have been if the four defectors had been, say, Bobby Orr, Bobby Hull, Phil Esposito and Rod Gilbert. What would the NHL have done then?

Right or wrong, the decision had been made. Certainly we were not looking at the ideal situation for turning back the Russian invasion. We did not have the best possible team available for the games; we would not be playing these games at the best possible time of year for Canadian professionals. The Russians train and practice eleven months of the year; many of our players had not been on the ice since April. Now we were expected to play very important games in very hot weather after only eighteen days of practice, and under extreme pressure. And finally, Team Canada was to be an all-star squad composed for the most part of individuals who had rarely, if ever, played together as teammates. Melding thirty-five individuals into one solid team in those eighteen days seemed like an impossible task.

Still, we could not make excuses. After all, we could have altered the situation ourselves by including the WHA players on Team Canada. We could have insisted on playing the series in mid-season, when NHL players traditionally round into their top physical condition. Or we could have had the Stanley Cup champions or some other single team face the Russian challenge.

The ironic part of the brouhaha over Bobby Hull's playing status for the series was that when plans for the games were announced, Hull's first comment was something to the effect that he would not play unless the money was right. Then he couldn't play, and suddenly he was a martyr for the cause. Bobby seemed to be playing the role perfectly.

August 9

I have finished my law exams, and now I'm trying to catch up on some back reading in the Canadian newspapers. Here it is the middle of the summer, and all over

Canada the swimming pools are still filled with bikinis, yet all you can read about in the papers is hockey. For the first time, hockey has emerged as a year-round sport.

Each day there are countless stories about the latest player signings by the WHA and the NHL, and they all seem to say pretty much the same thing: "Joe Highstick has signed a five-year, no-cut, no-trade contract with the Icemen for $1 million, a new pair of skates and two cars." There's the daily Bobby Hull story ("Will Bobby Join Team Canada?"), the daily Derek Sanderson story ("If They Want Me, I'll Be at Waikiki Beach") and the daily WHA vs. NHL story from the courtroom ("Judge Reserves Decision").

And, of course, there are four or five stories each day about the condition of Bobby Orr's injured left knee, which was operated on early in June and has been slow, fast or plain unable to respond to the prescribed post-operative care, depending upon the dateline of the report you read. In Boston the Bruins say: "Orr Recovery Slow, May Not Play Against Russians." In Toronto Bobby's lawyer, Alan Eagleson, says: "Orr May Be Ready for Game 4 in Vancouver." And at his camp in Orillia, Ontario, Orr himself says: "My Knee Is Fine."

Red Fisher, the sports editor of the *Montreal Star*, even flew over to Moscow to do a "Man on Gorki Street" interview with some Russian hockey fans and officials. One Russian wanted to know if Seth Martin would be playing goal for Team Canada, because he remembered Martin from his performances with Canadian national amateur teams throughout the sixties and figured Seth was still in top form. Martin retired a few years ago after an illustrious amateur career, but as far as the Russians and the Swedes were concerned, he was still Rocket Richard and Jean Beliveau and Gordie Howe all wrapped into one. The Russians idolized Martin, and the Russian goaltenders patterned their technique after Martin's technique. He was a great goaltender.

Another story that intrigued me concerned Alan Eagleson, representing Bobby Orr Enterprises, and Harold Ballard, the owner of the Toronto Maple Leafs, who paid seven hundred and fifty thousand dollars to Hockey Canada for television rights to the series. As Eagleson said: "I'm always prepared to put Bobby Orr's money where my mouth is."

Apparently, both Eagleson and Ballard were incensed when the only original offer of any size was a five-hundred-thousand-dollar bid tendered by MacLaren Advertising, which for years has controlled the television rights for the weekly "Hockey Night in Canada" telecasts from Montreal and Toronto. MacLaren later thought about increasing its offer, but Ballard and Eagleson countered by saying they were prepared to pay as much as one million dollars for the rights. They said that all profits, estimated at one million dollars, would be turned over to Hockey Canada and the pension fund of the NHL Players' Association.

I applaud Eagleson and Ballard for their initiative in this matter. People like to knock Eagleson, publicly and privately, for his actions, but in this case he acted for his clients, the Players' Association, and got some money for hockey. I doubt we would be playing this series if it wasn't for Eagleson.*

August 11

The hockey fever is really unbelievable. Everyone wants to become involved in the series somehow. Travel agencies throughout Canada set up attractive charter

---

* He does not represent me in any way.

packages, and all twenty-eight hundred available spots were sold out in a matter of hours. For less than six hundred and fifty dollars, hockey fans get round-trip air transportation from Toronto to Moscow, nine or ten nights in a Moscow hotel, all meals, daily sightseeing tours, all transfers and — most important — a reserved seat for all four hockey games in Moscow.

Department stores are conducting raffles and lotteries, and manufacturers everywhere are using game tickets as promotional come-ons. "Buy twenty boxes of nose-bleed powder and maybe you'll win two tickets for the Canada-Russia game in your hometown." One contest offers two free trips to Moscow to the person who picks the first Team Canada player to score against the Russians. The sponsors have a list of players on a sheet of paper, with a box alongside each name.

They even include me. A goaltender. Imagine me scoring a goal. No goalie has ever scored a goal in the NHL. Michel Plasse, who probably will be one of the Montreal goaltenders this year, scored a goal for Kansas City a few years ago when the other team — I think it was Oklahoma City — pulled its goaltender in the final moments, but that was a rare event. I doubt that I'll get very many votes, except Lynda's and mine.

August 12

Judging from the attitude of the people I have encountered the past few days, if we don't win this series 8 to 0 it will be a black mark for Canada. The newspapers, the television, the radio, the people in the street all say it has to be eight straight — and it will be eight straight or else. Anyone who dares suggest that Canada might lose a game to the Russians becomes an instant outcast, a heretic. We must not only win eight straight, but eight straight by big scores.

The people have developed a common bond with hockey players. While I was watching the Toronto Argonauts play a football game, the man next to me grabbed my hand, shook it, and said in a vigorous voice, "Try to do it for us." For us! He did not say it in a corny way. He said it with genuine emotion. Do it for us! For Canada! Later, I met someone I had played hockey with as a kid, and he said, almost as a warning, "I'm not going to talk to you again if you don't win eight straight."

Lynda went into a department store in Toronto and the clerk recognized my name on the charge plate. "Tell your husband he's got to beat those Russians," she told Lynda. Each day, I'm afraid, this series takes on greater overtones. It's frightening. Millions of Canadians are convinced that the Russians are villains, carpetbaggers, interlopers with the gall and the audacity to challenge us at our own game. It's our game. Go away.

The more I think about it, though, the more I can understand the mood of the Canadian people, because I am a Canadian, too. We are all frustrated. All of us. Hockey is an intimate part of our life in this country, and now the Russians are coming to challenge it. They are challenging Canada's right to be best at something. You may be the biggest hockey fan in Boston or New York or Chicago or Los Angeles, but I'm certain that you don't understand this. You must be a Canadian.

The first thing you must understand is the importance of hockey in Canada. It is a subject one rarely contemplates or articulates for very long. For the past few weeks, though, I have been thinking about what hockey really means to me. This is what happens when something so close to you is seriously challenged. The responses come slowly. The feelings develop gradually. And suddenly it all becomes an enormous thing.

Hockey is Canada's national game, and hockey interest far exceeds the combined interest in all the other sports played and seen in Canada.

The home games of the Canadian teams in the National Hockey League are broadcast and televised both locally and nationally. Year after year the No. 1–rated show on Canadian television has been Saturday's "Hockey Night in Canada" broadcast. The No. 2–rated show is the Wednesday broadcast of "Hockey Night in Canada." I doubt there's a Canadian anywhere who did not grow up listening to or watching the hockey games. I know I did.

I suspect the people in the United States realize how proud Canadians are of their hockey heritage because once they discover you are a Canadian they usually ask if you are a hockey player. It's the same thing in Europe. Throughout the world, in fact, hockey is absolutely synonymous with Canada. Even in Russia.

There is no such national, patriotic feeling for one particular sport in the United States. I have heard sober men argue into the night about whether baseball or football is No. 1 in the mind of the sports public. There is no reason for such argument in Canada.

You cannot compare this Canada-Russia hockey series with, say, the first global World Series of Baseball between the United States and Japan, because there simply isn't the feeling for baseball in the United States that there is for hockey in Canada. And it may not even be the No. 1 sport in its own country, since it is rivaled in popularity by football.

Canada has much to be proud of, but its twenty-two

million citizens also have a great capacity for self-depreciation, mostly, I think, because of the enormity of our neighbor, the United States.

Except for hockey, Canada has been singularly unsuccessful and ineffective in international athletics. We have a very difficult time every four years trying to put together a respectable team for the Olympic Games, and we very rarely win any gold medals. In fact, we rarely have *any* medal winners at all. Canadian professional football is regarded as minor league by United States' standards. Baseball is popular in Canada, but few Canadians ever become major leaguers (let me remind you that Ferguson Jenkins *is* from Chatham, Ontario) and we have only one major-league team, the Montreal Expos.

Canada's emotional affair with hockey perhaps can be compared only to the feelings that the people of some countries have for soccer. I remember being in Rome in 1970 when all of Italy went agog over the Italian team in the World Cup soccer championship. After years of frustration, the Italians were working their way to the finals and everything in Rome seemed to stand still.

The streets were empty when Italy upset Mexico and West Germany in classic games. After the games people streamed into the streets to celebrate, and the sound of blaring automobile horns echoed throughout the city. A nation was totally wrapped up in a sporting event. The Italians eventually lost to Brazil in the finals, but they returned home as heroes. They were saluted in the parliament and wined in the streets. Later, while the corks were still popping all over Rome, the parliament set up a committee to find out why the Italians lost in the finals.

As I see it, the series between the Canadian pros and the Russian amateurs is a classic confrontation unprecedented in sports because it involves two countries with opposite life styles which have developed hockey in almost total isolation from each other. The Canadians began playing hockey in the late 1800s; the Russians did not pick up the game until 1946. The two countries never met on the ice until 1954, when the Russians startled the world by upsetting a senior amateur team from Toronto in the World Tournament.

For Canada, this defeat bordered on a national disaster. Bordered, because senior amateur teams were composed of older players whose hockey careers were well behind them. They were members of the lunch-pail crowd at a plant or a construction yard who moonlighted by playing hockey. They were not future professionals by any means.

The next year the Penticton Vees from British Columbia rectified the situation by beating the Russians and winning the World Tournament. I can still remember listening to the games during the noon-hour recess at elementary school and hearing the commentators reassure us that if senior amateur teams could stay this close to the Russians, and even beat them, then there was no question that an NHL team would absolutely clobber the Soviets and the Swedes and everyone else in the world.

But gradually our senior amateur teams began to lose to the foreign competition. We won, we lost, but we were not worried; we knew we were the best. We had the NHL. Our worldwide reputation was at stake in these tournaments, however, and many people did not know there was such a thing as the NHL. As a Swedish hockey official said one year after another Canadian setback: "Your players wear CANADA across their uniforms, and this is the world championship. Now you want us to believe that you have even better players back home?" Who can blame them, since outside North America people assume that only the best athletes are chosen to perform for their countries in world tournaments.

In 1960 Canada even lost the Olympic gold medal to the United States, of all countries, and then three years later we finally woke up and decided that senior amateur teams were *not* good enough to beat the competition. At this point, the National Team was established, so that Canada's representatives in all international competitions would be younger players, most likely future pros, who would be able to combine their schooling with top-level hockey.

For most national players this was the only alternative to the NHL's monopoly on playing talent. Rather than play for only one team in hockey's only professional major league, young players had an option — playing for the National Team — which also gave them better bargaining power with the pro teams that owned the eventual rights to them. Before the National Team was organized, young prospective professionals complied with the wishes of their NHL team — or else they didn't play hockey.

Still, there was one major flaw with the National Team concept: in Canada the best hockey for sixteen-to twenty-year-olds is played outside the school, so the best players, if they did not belong to the National Team, had to forego their formal schooling in order to practice and play with the junior teams. As a result, many of them could not qualify for university-level schooling and, thus, were left without an alternative to playing pro hockey immediately, because NHL teams would offer them thousands of dollars to turn professional.

Not surprisingly, the NHL denigrated the National

Team. The NHL clubs said that playing for the National Team would handicap players' careers, for there would not be enough hitting or enough games or enough money. National Team players would lose development time, the NHL stated, and would not perform as well as their contemporaries who entered the pros directly. These factors ultimately discouraged many top amateur players, and as a result, very few of the best juniors ever opted for the National Team.

For the next seven years, the National Team suffered one frustrating, unhappy experience after another. It may have been the most maligned hockey team ever put together. It was given the job of winning the world championship or the Olympics, but it was hardly equipped to do either. The National Team always finished third or fourth or fifth. Never first. The Nationals might upset the Russians, but they would lose to Sweden or Czechoslovakia or Finland.

The people in Canada thought the Nationals would win the World Tournament in 1967 because Carl Brewer, the former star defenseman for the Toronto Maple Leafs of the NHL, had regained his amateur status and was on the team. But Brewer was injured during the championships and the Nationals lost again.

I joined the Nationals in 1969 after finishing my undergraduate career at Cornell. We finished fourth at Stockholm, beating the Finns twice, the Americans twice and losing twice to Sweden, Russia and Czechoslovakia. In other words, we beat no team of significance. So, again, everyone dumped on the Nationals.

Rather than sign a pro contract with the Montreal Canadiens, I decided to play for the Nationals in 1969–70 and also start law school at the University of Manitoba. Sammy Pollock, the general manager of the Canadiens, was taken aback when I told him of my plans. To his credit, he did not try to change my mind. Then mid-way through that season, the National Team finally went under for the last time. Sadly, this seemed a happy moment for everyone in Canada, except the people in Winnipeg, where the World Tournament was to have been staged that season. Without Canada in the tournament, the event was switched to Stockholm.

Most Canadians felt that it was better not to compete against the Russians and the Swedes and the Czechs than to play against them and get routed. We had run the gamut from college teams to senior amateur clubs to the National Team. We could no longer stomach losing and losing and losing. When you lose the world championship nine straight years, when you are defeated by Russian and Czech teams during informal tours, then there no longer is any reason for optimism. You must look elsewhere for a solution.

Most Canadians now believed that only an NHL team, or a team of NHL stars, should represent the country in world and Olympic competition. For almost three years, however, the conflict between professionalism and the amateur code crept into all discussions. Avery Brundage, the man whose iron hand ran the Olympics, and John "Bunny" Ahearne of Great Britain, the head of the International Hockey Federation, both adamantly refused to allow Canadian pros to compete against their not-so-lily-white amateurs.

For a long time there was not enough competitive feeling among the top amateur teams, such as Russia, Sweden and Czechoslovakia, to fight the decisions of Brundage and Ahearne, since the threat of losing Olympic eligibility far outweighed what other gains were possible. The Soviets, too, apparently felt they had not established enough superiority to turn their backs on the World Tournament and the Olympics and challenge the

Canadian pros for outright world supremacy. But soon things began to change.

After twenty years of incredible growth, the Soviet hockey program began to settle into a period of mediocrity. The Russians continued to win some Olympic gold medals and the World Tournament, but not as consistently as they once had. In 1972, in fact, Czechoslovakia upset the Soviets for the world championship, although we all know the Russians are the superior hockey players.

Now the Russians realized that winning more Olympic medals and world championships would not be that significant if their game stagnated at the same time. As Kirill Romensky of the Soviet Hockey Federation said: "There is nothing more for us to learn from the competition. It is time we move on to better opposition so we can improve our skills and learn more about the game."

Sorry, Mr. Brundage. Sorry, Mr. Ahearne.

And so, after very brief negotiations in Prague last March, Canada and Russia agreed to play the first World Series of Hockey. Professionals against amateurs. The best of two worlds.

August 13

All day long, hockey players have been checking into Sutton Place, a luxury high-rise hotel here in Toronto, for the official start of Team Canada's training camp. We're now off to our first meeting with Coach Harry Sinden and his assistant, John Ferguson, the onetime policeman for the Montreal Canadiens and a teammate of mine for a couple of weeks at the end of the 1970–71 season and in the Stanley Cup play-offs. I am quite skeptical about Fergy's selection.

It is not just that Fergy has had no prior coaching

experience. Superficially, or at least judging from the tone of his statements, it seems that Fergy has been picked strictly to instill an overly aggressive style of play in Team Canada's game. His success in the NHL stemmed largely from his ability to play a rough, vicious game that intimidated his rivals to the point where they began to worry more about their physical safety than the game they were supposed to be playing.

For instance, Fergy usually was assigned to cover Rod Gilbert when the Canadiens played against the Rangers, and early in the game he never objected to taking a high-sticking or a charging penalty if he thought it would serve to preoccupy Gilbert's attentions for the rest of the night. Another time, he told an opposing forward with a good goal-scoring touch that he intended to knock him into the fourth row of seats the first time he handled the puck. The poor guy was puck-shy all night.

I don't think we should use such tactics against the Russians. It's not the right approach. As our players will find out, the Russians are extremely strong and tend to disdain rough, vicious play, although they are more than capable of playing that way. We would only end up in the penalty box, and one of the strongest aspects of the Russian game is the power play. So, it seems to me that Fergy is not going to be the ideal assistant for Harry Sinden.

Here is the roster:

Goaltenders: Tony Esposito of Chicago, Eddie Johnston of Boston, and me. E. J. was named as a last-minute replacement for Gerry Cheevers.

Defensemen: Bobby Orr and Don Awrey of Boston, Brad Park and Rod Seiling of New York, Guy Lapointe and Serge Savard of Montreal, Jocelyn Guevremont and Dale Tallon of Vancouver, Gary Bergman of Detroit, Pat Stapleton and Bill White of Chicago, and Brian Glennie of Toronto. Orr still is recuperating from his knee operation and may not check in for another week or so. I doubt he will be ready to play until the first game in Moscow on September 22, if then.

Center: Phil Esposito of Boston, Stan Mikita of Chicago, Gilbert Perreault of Buffalo, Marcel Dionne and Red Berenson of Detroit, Jean Ratelle of New York, and Bobby Clarke of Philadelphia. Clarke by the way, showed up wearing what Red Fisher of the *Montreal Star* called his Flin Flon summer suit: a T-shirt, Levis and sneakers. No socks.

Left wing: Dennis Hull of Chicago, Peter and Frank Mahovlich of Montreal, Jean-Paul Parise of Minnesota, Paul Henderson of Toronto, Vic Hadfield of New York, and Richard Martin of Buffalo.

Right wing: Rod Gilbert of New York, Yvan Cournoyer of Montreal, Wayne Cashman of Boston, Ron Ellis of Toronto, Mickey Redmond of Detroit, and Bill Goldsworthy of Minnesota.

Joe Sgro of Toronto and Frosty Forristall of Boston are the trainers, and Tommy Naylor of Toronto is the equipment man. Frosty provides a Yankee touch to Team Canada. Indeed, he is our only American. The Lone Ranger, even though he has been around Canadian hockey players so long that he now thinks like a Canadian. If things go bad we can blame it on him.

Harry spoke briefly and to the point. He stressed how important the series will be, and he stressed that we will have to win. We have to beat the Russians. He said he will not hold us to a strict curfew but that he expects us to use our own good judgment. If we have any problems, we are to see Harry or Fergy at once. If we have to fulfill a business commitment, they will make the arrangements for us. If anyone wants to go home next weekend, they will provide a round-trip ticket. Things like that. Obviously, Team Canada plans to be very accommodating to the players. There's no doubt we will go first-class.

August 14

Like most people, I have to wonder how seriously we players will approach hockey practice in the middle of the summer, when we normally are out at hockey school, or on the golf course, on the tennis court, or just plain sunbathing at poolside. Will we be only half serious and force Sinden and Ferguson to get tough in the two-a-day workouts? Or will we be totally serious and completely committed to the job of beating the Russians? We probably won't know the answer for another week or ten days.

Harry and Fergy have set up some obvious line combinations for the time being, though they could become permanent. The New York line of Ratelle, Gilbert and Hadfield that devastated the NHL in general and Ken Dryden in particular last season (they averaged a couple of goals a game against me) most likely will remain intact throughout the series. Another line has Phil Esposito centering for Frank Mahovlich and Yvan Cournoyer. The Russian goalies will hardly like facing that threesome; indeed, Esposito scored 66 goals last year, Cournoyer had 47, and Mahovlich had 43. That's 156 goals, according to my computer, or just 44 less than all the Philadelphia Flyers managed to score a year ago.

One other line has Bobby Clarke centering for Ron Ellis and Paul Henderson. Norm Ullman works between Ellis and Henderson for the Maple Leafs during the regular schedule, and Clarke plays much the same way as Ullman. They are like three buzz saws as they scoot around the ice harassing people with their tenacious forechecking and strong backchecking. I have a feeling they will be a big surprise for the Russians.

August 15

I read an interesting article last month in the *Manchester Guardian* about David Hemery, a graduate of Boston University who won the four-hundred-meter hurdles championship for Great Britain at the 1968 Olympics in Mexico City. Hemery was a dark horse in 1968, and now, in August, despite his being the defending champion, he is just as much an underdog for the 1972 Games at Munich.

Hemery said that he always has been the kind of hurdler who has not shown good practice times but that never really concerns him. He figures that when the competition forces him into a good time he will have enough physical reserve to produce it. Why? Because of his training program:

> I run mile after mile after mile every day, because someday I know it will be beneficial in a race. Sure, it may not be helpful for a week or two or six months or even five years, but sometime that work — running up those hills, hurdling an extra barrier — will be the reason why I win a race.

As I read about Hemery's approach to conditioning, I realized he was right, and I decided to apply it to my own training regimen. Now, as we work out in Maple Leaf Gardens, my job as I see it is to get myself into condition. I want to strengthen my legs. I want to sharpen my reflexes. I want to get reaccustomed to the extra weight of my goaltending equipment. The heck with the current results. The heck with the shots that are flying by me from all angles. I'll stop them later. I hope.

[22]

I'm breaking in a new set of pads and having trouble getting used to them. They are very stiff and feel awkward and heavy on my legs. They also are too long. As a result, my mobility is restricted and I am not getting to some easy shots that I should be handling without any trouble at all. The ice in the Gardens is slow and bumpy, and the puck is rolling on the shooters. So a lot of shots are coming very high at me, and flying past my head.

Right now I'm playing more with an eye towards safety than stopping the puck. This is a bad approach for any goaltender and something I'll have to overcome very soon. In order to stop a puck traveling at speeds greater than one hundred miles an hour, you cannot worry about your physical well-being. You must concentrate fully on stopping the puck and forget everything else.

August 16

Phil Esposito now is centering a line for Jean-Paul Parise and Wayne Cashman, while Stan Mikita has moved in between Frank Mahovlich and Yvan Cournoyer. Parise and Cashman are known primarily as diggers; they storm into the corner and usually come out with the puck. Cashman plays on the same line with Espo in Boston and probably gets an assist on seventy-five percent of Phil's goals.

Espo scores a majority of his goals on hard, quick wrist shots from less than twenty feet outside the net. He simply plants his immovable body in one spot and waits patiently for Cashman or Ken Hodge (his other wing in Boston) to control the puck in the corner and pass it out to him. Then, before the goalie can move, Espo fires it past him. Against Boston I try not to concern myself too much with the actions of Cashman and

Hodge in the corners, and instead, focus most of my attention on Esposito the moment he steps into the so-called slot. All goalies know this secret; if we didn't pay attention to Espo he would score one hundred and twenty-five goals.

Parise, who has never been a great scorer, and Cashman seem to be ideal wings for Phil. Cashman also is one of the comedians on the team. The other day one of the other Bruins told us a typical Cashman story. It seems that Wayne had some trouble with the police last spring after the Bruins won the Stanley Cup, and they brought him down to the station house.

"Okay, you can make one phone call," an officer told him.

Cash staggered over to the phone, dialed some numbers, and in a couple of seconds began to mumble incoherently. Then he slammed down the phone. A few minutes later there was a knock on the door and the officer went to open it. A little Chinese man stood there.

"Yes?" said the officer.

"Chinese food for Mr. Wayne Cashman," the delivery-man said.

Cashman had ordered enough won-ton soup and sweet-and-sour pork and egg foo yong to feed all the overnight inmates and their keepers.

August 17

Good news this morning. In yesterday's practice Yvan Cournoyer deflected one of Dennis Hull's bullets and the puck shot into Brad Park's face with a sickening thud. For what seemed like the longest time, Brad lay motionless on the ice. Then he was half-carried, half-dragged to the dressing room, and from there he was rushed to the hospital. We were all certain that his cheekbone was shattered.

"No break, thank God," Sinden told us before practice. "Only a bruise." Later, Brad came by the dressing room to pick up some things. "All I want to do now is go home and have a couple of beers," Park said. Sinden laughed. "Have three — on me," he said.

We all hope Brad will be passing out cigars when he returns. His wife, Gerry, is overdue with their first child.

August 18

It's pretty obvious now that Sinden and Ferguson will not try to change our playing styles just for this series. On the ice they have told us to play our own game and not rearrange anything. They are right, too. We can't play the Russians' game and expect to beat them. We can only beat them playing our own game at its best.

Also, I owe John Ferguson an apology. I think I've misunderstood how Fergy used to play. He had an overwhelming drive to win and it manifested itself in an aggressive approach to a game. He was not a great shooter or puckhandler, so to contribute he played a rough game. His inclusion is an attempt to instill this drive to win in our players, though not necessarily by using Fergy's playing style. The more I think about it, the more I understand how he can help us. Peter Mahovlich, for instance, always seems to play better when there is someone around to prod him. In Montreal, Fergy used to chase Peter around the ice during practice — growling all the time — and his gung-ho tactics helped turn Peter from an average player into a thirty-five-goal scorer. Sorry, Fergy.

Sinden and Ferguson are managing the two-a-day

workouts beautifully; the ninety-minute morning exercise and the sixty-minute afternoon drill have just enough seriousness and levity to make for interesting times. We are not exercising or practicing any differently than NHL teams normally do, but we are training with an obvious air of enthusiasm that is not often found at most training camps.

Right from the start, all the players have expended tremendous, concentrated energy during our periods on the ice. It takes only two or three great players who are working hard — a Mahovlich, an Esposito, a Park — to make the others get to work. The general attitude seems to be: "Who am I not to work?" if these great players put out.

There seems to be another motive behind the performances of some of the so-called nonstars. They want to prove to the stars that they are good players, that they deserve the respect of the stars. I know this may sound corny, but it's true. What it has come down to is that everyone in camp wants to be one of the best of the best, and the only way to do that is by working hard against the best.

August 19

Week No. 1 is over, thank goodness, and I'm glad we are not playing the Russians tomorrow night. I'm certainly not close to being ready; then again, all I wanted to do this week was get in shape. I think I did. I know my legs feel strong, and I have lost a few pounds. The soreness and the stiffness that come with exercise after a long layoff seem to have worn off. I may have disappointed my teammates this week by missing so many

shots, but I'm sure that next week will be more productive in a puck-stopping sense.

When a goaltender does not impress his teammates,
they rarely, if ever, say anything to him. In that regard,
goaltenders are practically immune from criticism. But
you can always sense the team's displeasure. On the
other hand, when a goaltender rallies his abilities and
begins to regain his form, his teammates start to say
little things to him, like "Welcome back" or "And where
have you been?"

It is a great feeling to own the respect of others,
particularly the respect of the best talents in your field.
Maybe I don't have their respect right now, after six
days on the ice, but I hope I will have it in a few days.

August 21

I have to laugh at something Don Awrey of the Bruins
said to Yvan Cournoyer of the Canadiens during practice one day last week. "We're buddy-buddy teammates
now, friend, but the minute we land back in Canada on
October 1 we'll be old enemies again. Don't forget it."
Indeed, one surprising aspect of the first week of practice was the absolute lack of temper flare-ups — like
high sticks — between individuals who go out of their
way to knock each other upside down during the regular
season.

For instance, Brad Park wrote some uncomplimentary
things about Phil Esposito in his book, and Esposito
suggested that Park should spell his name backwards.
Yet last week they were on the ice together, passing the
puck to each other and forgetting any previous hostilities
for now. Many outsiders probably thought the coaches

[27]

would have to prevail upon the players to ignore their old rivalries and play together as a team. Maybe the coaches thought so, too. But once you are on the same team and get to know your old rivals, you find out that they are pretty decent guys.

As of right now, harmony reigns on Team Canada. Peace. It's wonderful.

August 22

No matter how interesting the coaches try to make practice sessions they basically are boring. You eventually get very tired of stops and starts. Huh! So tonight we played our first intrasquad game. Like all early season exhibitions, the offense predominated, and in the end fatigue was the winner. I played fifty minutes and let in six goals. Not a very impressive performance, to be sure. And the Russians will be here in ten days.

August 24

Peter Mahovlich and Dale Tallon had a friendly golf match today — or was it friendly? Peter plays to a floating handicap, anything between about 8 and 28, depending upon his competition, while Dale shoots 72s on his worst days. Anyway, Dale gave Peter a hatful of strokes, and when they finally came to the eighteenth green there was a great deal of money riding on Peter's straight-in putt from about five feet. The kind of putt that Jack Nicklaus always makes with his eyes closed.

Peter inspected the putt from every imaginable angle. He gave it the plumb-bob treatment. He checked the grain. He checked the location of the Atlantic Ocean and Lake Ontario. He inquired about the wind-chill factor in the Klondike. He even spit shined his golf ball and wiped the face of his putter. He did everything right — except make the putt. The ball didn't come within two feet of the hole.

"Peter," I said, "it's very difficult to make a putt when your hands are wrapped around your own neck instead of the putter."

August 26

For almost a month now all I've read about in the newspapers and heard about on television is the series between Canada and the Soviet Union. Still, it always has seemed pretty distant, pretty remote. September 2 was a long way away.

This afternoon, though, the immediacy of the series hit home for the first time as I watched the great ceremony and pageantry of the opening of the Olympic Games in Munich. To me, it was much like the opening of the international hockey competitions. Suddenly, my thoughts switched from other things to the Russians. To Game 1 next week. I could feel the nervousness down to my legs. I shivered for a few seconds. My heart seemed to be beating faster. Pressure had hit me.

Then we had another intrasquad game, with about seventy-five hundred fans looking on, in Maple Leaf Gardens. I played sixty minutes this game, gave up only four goals, and felt much better. Now, if I can keep up this same rate of improvement, I'll be ready for the Russians.

August 27

I did not see the Russian scouts peeking around at the game last night, so I guess they have returned to Moscow to tell their players how good we are. Or maybe how bad we are. The two of them, Boris Kulagin and Arkady Tcherneshev, had watched our practices and squad games, and they seemed to make notes about everything that happened. If, say, Frank Mahovlich takes 1.96538 seconds to go from blue line to blue line, I'm sure the Russians know it by now. It was really funny: if I missed an easy shot, I found myself looking up to see if they were making a note.

I gather that the Russians take the same approach to hockey scouting as football scouts do in the United States. They will probably feed all the information into a computer and come up with a way to stop Phil Esposito when he has the puck on his stick twenty feet in front of the net. If they do, I hope they'll give me a copy of the computer print-out at the end of the series. Anytime.

Tcherneshev was a jovial sort, but Kulagin never cracked a smile. One night some Canadian scouts took Tcherneshev to see *The Godfather* at a movie theater in Toronto. Tcherneshev said he had read the book and wanted the scouts to know that there is no Mafia in Russia.

August 28

The big, final push is under way at last. This morning we received our itineraries for the trip to Montreal, and this afternoon we were given our official Team Canada traveling clothes — a blue blazer with a breast-pocket crest of a large maple leaf with TEAM CANADA inscribed on it and two pairs of silver-gray slacks.

We will be leaving for Montreal on two separate jets Friday morning, September 1. The NHL owners understandably do not want their thirty-five all-stars flying around on one plane, although Peter Mahovlich wondered what would happen if they collided. Once in Montreal, we will practice at the Forum and attend a brief reception atop the mall in Place Ville Marie. After that, though, no one will be bothering us until the Russians show up at the Forum Saturday night.

August 29

John McLellan and Bob Davidson, respectively the coach and the chief scout for the Toronto Maple Leafs, went to Russia and scouted the Soviet players for us. Poor John and Bob flew twelve or thirteen hours to Moscow, then were immediately put on the overnight train for Leningrad. What they watched in Leningrad put them to sleep. The Russian goalie, twenty-year-old Vladislav Tretiak, was beaten for eight goals in one game, and his teammates apparently were tripping all over themselves. Needless to say, McLellan and Davidson did not come back with glowing reports.

But I'm not convinced. It is easy to be unimpressed when you watch someone doing things that your own experience tells you is wrong. By North American standards, which McLellan and Davidson are used to, the Russians pass too much, don't shoot enough, and are too small. By European standards, though, these are not weaknesses. Who is right? We'll find out soon, but we shouldn't take the reports from Leningrad too seriously.

We played our final intrasquad game and it was telecast across Canada. I worked thirty minutes and did not allow any goals. I feel confident at last — and ready.

August 30

My middle finger is swollen, very blue and terribly painful. At practice today Gilbert Perreault took a shot from about thirty-five feet out that completely fooled me because it was not as hard or as fast as his shots normally are. The puck struck the end of the middle finger on my catching (left) hand.

I have been applying ice for hours now without any results. The X rays proved negative, thank goodness, but I'm really worried about what effect the injury will have on Saturday night. I think I deserve to play Game 1, not only because it will be in Montreal, where I play all season, but also because I think I have been extremely sharp for the last week.

All of us desperately want to play on Saturday night because it is Game 1 of a historic event. It will mean so much to be one of the best seventeen and two — that is, seventeen skaters and two goaltenders. But despite my hopes and my desires, I certainly will not even dress for the game unless I feel my finger will not affect my play.

The injury is in a very bad place because the catching hand is a valuable instrument, and it must function correctly. Also, when you do have an injury, no matter where it is, you are subconsciously aware of it during a game. When you make a movement that involves the injured part of your body, you tend to hold back ever so slightly, which could be the difference between making a save or permitting a goal.

As I sit here nursing my finger, I am watching a show called "Sportsbeat '72." John Robertson, a sports columnist for the *Montreal Star*, and Brian Conacher, a former National Team and NHL player, are having a debate about the series. Four or five days ago, Robertson predicted in print that Russia would win the series 6–2, saying they would split the four games in Canada and sweep the four in Moscow.

Robertson offers several reasons for his prediction, starting with conditioning. He says that the Russians play and train eleven months of the year and have been in serious training for this series since July 1. Besides that, Robertson insists that the Russians will be motivated by a nationalistic drive that Canadian pros have never had to encounter. Then he blames the rift between the NHL and the WHA for costing Team Canada four valuable players, and finally, he states there is too much pressure on Team Canada.

Very interesting. Robertson, though, attempts to mechanize something that you really cannot mechanize. He takes arbitrary divisions, such as conditioning, motivation, nationalism and pressure, gives them arbitrary weights, adds up the figures, and comes out with Russia 6, Canada 2. Certainly Robertson's factors do have weight, but I think there are other factors with as much or even more weight — and some of them may be more favorable to Team Canada than Russia.

Certainly I agree with his thoughts about conditioning, but I disagree with his feelings about the WHA defections. Personally I think there is only one WHA player who would be of any help to us against the Russians: Bobby Hull. The others are great players, but we already have thirty-five.

Motivation? I'm not sure. The typical NHL player grew up harboring the idea that the Stanley Cup is the key event in a hockey player's life, but I think our players will adjust to the idea that beating Russia is more important than any Stanley Cup. I don't think you can predict when someone's motivation will surface. Motivation does not show too early. Talk to our players and they will give you the basic public spiel: "Yeah, I want to play and win for my country." But they probably don't feel that way right now because the games are still in the distance. Those verbalized feelings will become a reality, however, on September 2 at 8 p.m. in the Montreal Forum. Motivation will be no problem for Team Canada. I think we will thrive on pressure.

I know why Robertson made his prediction, though. Everyone in Canada is saying eight straight. Robertson would be lost in the crowd if he said the same thing, and John never likes to be lost in the crowd. So he says 6–2 for the Russians — and there he is on "Sportsbeat '72." It does make interesting reading and listening, if for the wrong reasons.

While I agree with Robertson's theory that the Soviets tend to avoid competition in sports until they know they can make an acceptable showing, I also agree with Brian Conacher, who suggests that the Soviets are prepared to lose this series and plan to use it as a learning device for their younger players. I think this series is an exception for the Russians. They obviously realize that their rate of development has slowed down tremendously and that a series with the Canadian professionals is the only way to begin another spurt and to revitalize their program.

Conacher says that whatever the result, the Soviets will get more from the games than the Canadians. Again I agree with him. But we will see that the Russians have many, many things that North American teams would do well to adopt: their passing plays, their conditioning programs, their defensive tactics.

The Russians have proved they are more progressive in their attitudes and approaches towards sports. They have shown an amazing ability to optimize strengths, minimize weaknesses, and build solid programs. North American hockey programs are haphazard in comparison. We can learn a lot from the Russians.

If the Russians win, well, they beat the best so now they are the best. If they lose, then they can say they had an opportunity to play against professionals and to study their techniques. But we Canadians find ourselves on a one-way street. We must score an overwhelming 8 to 0 victory. Anything less will be a shattering defeat.

Now Conacher says that "goaltending will be the difference" and "Dryden will be the great equalizer." Thank you, Brian, but what has happened to your memory? You remember what happened in Vancouver almost three years ago? You were a teammate that night when the Russians ripped nine goals past me. Nine goals. Either you have a bad memory or my goaltending has improved. I hope it is the latter.

I have to laugh at the way all the experts categorize the components of a hockey game and arbitrarily assign a winner to each one. The general consensus seems to be this:

> Shooting — Canada
> Passing — Russia
> Hockey Sense — Canada
> Conditioning — Russia
> Goaltending — Canada

So, in the end, Tony Esposito, Eddie Johnston and I are being counted on to provide the big, extra edge. But who is to say that our goaltending is any better? I would agree that in general our overall goaltending is better. We should not be looking just at the general situation, however. In a short series, all that's necessary is for one goaltender to get hot; the fact that he has no adequate backup man is of little consequence, unless, of course, he gets injured. And who is to say that goaltending superiority — if we have that — will be a weightier factor than conditioning or passing? My worst games in the NHL generally have been against the New York Rangers, who have the best passing attack in the league. Their short, crisp plays around the goal mouth usually leave me in the third row of the seats. So what will happen against the Russians, who probably pass the puck better than the Rangers ever dreamed? All this theorizing really means very little.

We watched films of the Russians today for a couple of hours. Believe me, they are a good hockey team.

August 31

The Russians arrived in Montreal at nine o'clock last night, and at nine o'clock this morning they were on the ice at the suburban St. Laurent Arena for what Coach Vsevolod Bobrov called a "light drill." Light drill? For the next ninety minutes the twenty-seven Russian players skated nonstop through an involved series of exercises that most Canadians had never witnessed before. The Russians restrict their technical practice to game-situation drills and intrasquad scrimmages; they shun the carefree shoot, shoot, shoot type of program that dominates Canadian hockey practices.

No Russian player sat down during the workout or

leaned over the boards to catch his breath or took a squirt of water. Bobrov had them doing push-ups off the ice, body rolls on it, and various other drills that chill the body but not the spirit — like somersaults on skates.

In one drill, a three-man forward line moved swiftly (the only way the Russians move) up the ice, criss-crossing all the while and crisply passing the puck without mistake. At the end of that play, one of the forwards turned around, skated in reverse, and played defense-man while his normal linemates tried to beat him on a two-on-one break. Tricky, and very practical.

After the morning workout the Russian players re-turned to their hotel for lunch, a long afternoon nap, and then some sightseeing. By 8 P.M., though, they were back on the ice at the Arena for a shorter sixty-minute workout, during which they seemed to do all the things they needed ninety minutes to do in the morning. After that it was back to the hotel again. Someone asked one of the Russian interpreters if the players were tired because of the two workouts and the seven-hour time difference between Moscow and Montreal. After all, at 8 P.M. in Montreal, it is 3 A.M. the next day in Moscow.

No, the interpreter said. For the last two weeks the Russian players had been living on Montreal time. They did not have to adjust their watches or their bodies when they landed.

September 1

We left Toronto and flew into Montreal in time to see most of the Russian team's practice at the Forum. As I watched them skate around the rink, not looking any-thing like a great hockey team, I remembered something that I had read once about what the Russians did to John Thomas, the American world's record high jumper, a certain gold medal winner in the 1960 Olympics at Rome. For days, two obscure Russian high jumpers, Valery Brumel and Robert Shavlakadze, studied all of Thomas's workouts, and afterwards they asked him for tips about jumping. So Thomas would watch them struggle over the bar at very low heights and then help them with their form.

Oh, did the Russians psych Thomas. Came the high-jump finals and there was Shavlakadze pulling down the gold medal, Brumel finishing with the silver, and Thomas going home almost empty-handed, with only the bronze. Maybe they are doing the same thing to us.

In the morning workout Tretiak, the goaltender who gave up those eight goals the night McLellan and Davidson scouted him in Leningrad, kept backing into his net and stabbing helplessly at the puck. The forwards seemed to shoot off the wrong foot; their shots looked like marshmallows. And their defensemen appeared to be big and slow; every time they tried to change direction they practically fell on their face. At least, I thought that's how it looked — or did I just want to see it that way?

Psychological warfare, they call it. The Russians always seem to play their roles perfectly. Look bad in practice, dupe the other guy, then tell him how good he is. Bobby Orr walked into the Forum, took a seat in the stands, and a moment later some Soviet attaché brought a handful of papers to him for his autograph. "For the players," the man said, and Bobby dutifully signed them.

Bobby himself studied Tretiak's movements in the goal — particularly his apparent weakness with the catching glove — and decided that Dennis Hull, Phil Esposito and everyone else would have a field day against him. To a man, we now were supremely confident that we would beat the Russians pretty easily.

Still, it appears to me that the Russian shooters have improved considerably since I last faced them almost three years ago. Their big play still seems to be the goal-mouth pass. They like to maneuver the puck in close with a series of short, crisp passes and then slide it across the goal mouth to an uncovered wing who has a practically empty net to shoot at. There is no more difficult play for a goaltender to stop. Our defensemen should not allow the Russian forwards to work this play; to stop it, they will have to collapse around the goal and not permit them to penetrate too closely.

The Montreal defensemen never were able to do this last year in games against the New York Rangers, and as a result, the Rangers handled us easily. Vic Hadfield set up permanent residence at the corner of the crease to my right, and he must have scored seven goals against me from that spot. Of course, my Montreal defensemen also had to worry about the Rangers shooting the puck past me from thirty-five feet. When a team has an arsenal of weapons and can beat you from thirty-five feet or three feet with equal ease, it makes the goal-mouth pass even more difficult to defend against.

From what I know about the Russians, they beat you easily from three feet but don't beat you too often from thirty-five feet. This should make it somewhat easier for Team Canada's defensemen.

While the Russians' hockey skills did not impress us in the workout, their physical condition did. As we had been warned, they were in fantastic shape and didn't even work up a sweat. Tretiak startled Eddie Johnston with his acrobatic routines whenever the puck was at the opposite end of the rink. He would do a belly flop onto the ice, kick out both legs, then pop back onto his feet again — and repeat the act eight or ten times. "Can't you just imagine Gump Worsley doing that?" E. J. said. Or Ken Dryden, for that matter.

After finishing his workout, Tretiak stayed at the Forum to watch our practice. He looks much like a young Stan Mikita. His cheeks have a reddish look that someday will be dulled by the daily use of a razor blade. He is apparently the star product of a crash program to develop outstanding goaltenders. The Soviet Union has produced few good goaltenders, mostly because there are so few games in Russia where an athlete has to react and catch something. Most NHL goaltenders have a baseball background of some sort — I even played short-stop as late as my freshman year at Cornell — but there is no baseball in the Soviet Union. I suspect that Tretiak is very quick with his feet because soccer is a popular sport in the Soviet Union and all youngsters participate in some type of soccer program.

Tretiak said he began as a forward when he started to play hockey at the age of seven because his mother was a forward. She played bandy, a game played outdoors on ice with curved sticks and a small ball — almost like field hockey. He became a goaltender at the age of nine and in recent years had studied films of Eddie Giacomin and Jacques Plante and tried to pattern his style after both of them. "I also would like to have the self-confidence of Viktor Konovalenko," Tretiak said. Konovalenko, known in Russia as the Little Bear, was the star goaltender of the Soviet Union's Olympic and world championship teams throughout the sixties.

As he talked, Tretiak studied the Team Canada shooters. Once he interrupted his conversation to say, "Esposito manages to make the shot without any preparation, doesn't he?" Yes, Vladislav, he does. Tretiak also laughed aloud when his interpreter asked why he had played so badly and had given up eight goals in the game that McLellan and Davidson had scouted in Leningrad.

"That night," he said, "was not one of my best. But you must understand that I was getting married the next day, and, oh, my mind was away from the hockey game."

After we finished our workout, Sinden named the lineup for the opening game. All things considered, I don't think there were any surprises. Tony Esposito and I were selected as the goaltenders, but neither Harry nor Fergy gave any indication which one of us would start the game. In fact, they suggested we might split the game down the middle.

On defense, Brad Park and Gary Bergman will form one tandem, Don Awrey and Rod Seiling another, and Guy Lapointe will be the swingman. Bergman has been one of the surprise players in the camp, according to all the so-called experts. Now people are saying they never knew he was such a good hockey player. How many experts have watched Bergman closely the last few years at Detroit? When you play for a team that doesn't make the play-offs, then you are automatically overlooked. Bergie is a complete defenseman; in fact, he may be the best shot-blocker in hockey.

Up front, Esposito will center the No. 1 line for Cournoyer and Frank Mahovlich; Ratelle will work with his New York linemates Hadfield and Gilbert; Clarke will play with Ellis and Henderson; and Peter Mahovlich, Mickey Redmond, and Red Berenson will be the spares. Bobby Clarke is another player, like Bergman, who has recently convinced the experts that he is a standout hockey player. The players knew that all along.

Before we left the ice, Red Berenson, one of the centers, told Sinden and Ferguson to get lost for a couple of minutes because he had something he wanted to say privately to the players. "Look," Red said to us as we gathered in a circle near the net, "we have thirty-five outstanding hockey players here right now but only nineteen will be dressing tomorrow night. It's no disgrace not to be playing. Let's not be disillusioned. Someone had to make the choices — and it was a thankless, impossible job. Let's not be disappointed. Let's not blast the coaches. This is a team of thirty-five men. Let's keep it that way."

After our meeting, I went downtown to the hotel, had a short nap, and then took a cab to my apartment in Notre Dame de Grace for a quiet, peaceful dinner with Lynda. The cabbies in Montreal are ridiculous. One of them turned around and said to me, "If you guys don't win you'll never live it down." It seems that we have twenty-two million threats hanging over our heads.

About 8:30 P.M. I returned to the hotel and turned on the television in my room. Suddenly I remembered the night I turned on the television set in Boston — the night before the seventh game of the Canadiens-Bruins play-off in 1971. I was nervous, and all I wanted to do was relax. So what was on the screen? The "Boston Bruins Highlights" show. Well, they never highlight defensive plays or great saves on such programs, believe me. They are all offense, all goals, all red lights. This show featured the highlights of the three Boston-Montreal play-off games played that week.

The Bruins had scored fifteen goals in the three games (they won two of them, by the way) and now I had a chance to relive each one of them in A) regular action, B) slow-motion replay, C) stop action, and D) slow-motion, stop action. It was hardly a confidence booster on the eve of my biggest game as a pro. It looked as though everything they shot at me ended up in the net. The highlights never showed me making a save — not even an easy one. (Somehow I recovered from that television debacle, though, and we upset the Bruins the next afternoon in the Boston Garden. They scored only two goals against me. I've often wondered what they showed on their next highlights program.)

While I was relaxing in my Montreal hotel room, alternately watching the Olympics and a football exhibition between the Detroit Lions and the Baltimore Colts, the Russian players were at a local theater. They had set out to see a cowboy movie but ended up at *The Godfather*.

Incidentally, Boris Spassky lost his World Chess Championship to Bobby Fischer today. Spassky phoned in his resignation. A couple of guys at the Forum were joking that maybe the Russian hockey players would call dial-a-defeat and phone in a forfeit for tomorrow night's game. Nobody laughed.

September 2

At last it's here. The days and months of worry are over. In a few hours we'll find out just how good the Russians are. And just how good we are. It's 3:30 P.M. now, four and one-half hours from game time, and I'm feeling a lot more relaxed that I ever thought I would be. We had a team meeting and a brief skate at the Forum this morning, and Sinden told me that I will be starting the game. He said that he'd like to alternate Tony Esposito and myself in each of the first two games, with both of us playing a total of sixty minutes. Considering the circumstances, it might not be a bad plan. It's above ninety degrees outside right now and the Forum probably will be warmer than a sauna; the emotion of the game and our short conditioning program all will combine to produce great fatigue. But Harry said his decision will depend on the game situation at the time. In international hockey you cannot warm up a fresh goaltender during a period. So, if things go well, I'll probably play forty minutes tonight and Tony will finish up, then Tony will play the first forty minutes in Toronto on Monday night and I will finish up. I hope things go well.

I don't think goalies like to play only part of a game. I know I don't, unless, of course, I'm injured. It's not that easy for a goalie to sit on the bench for part of a game and then come out onto the ice and get actively involved in that game. There's not only the physical problem but also the psychological problem of having to perform up to the standard of the departed goaltender. No matter what, you have very little time to overcome the negative pressure of switching during the game.

Rick Noonan, who used to be a trainer for the National Team and who is helping the Russian trainers here in Canada, told me that the Russian players drink Coca-Cola like it's going out of style. I guess it's nothing for a Valery Kharlamov, say, to have six or seven Cokes at breakfast, six or seven Cokes at lunch and six or seven Cokes at dinner, not to mention the Cokes he drinks in between. The Russians like ice cream, too; one of them bought a double scoop in Place Ville Marie but the top scoop fell off and landed on his shirt.

One of the Russians asked about the commotion a couple of blocks from their hotel late last night. No commotion! A holocaust! Fire broke out in the Blue Bird Club, a Country and Western hangout downtown. At last count, thirty-seven bodies had been found in the burned-out wreckage.

I went for a brief skate myself this morning, a definite departure from my normal game-day routine. With the Canadiens, if a goaltender wants to test his skates during the morning skate, he must don his complete set of goalie's equipment. So, I rarely go for the morning exercise. Today it was a fun twenty minutes or so. I imagined that I was Bobby Orr and Phil Esposito and Frank Mahovlich and Rod Gilbert — all four of them — and skated around "blasting" the puck at the other goalies. It was nice to see how the other half lives for a change.

At the morning meeting, Sinden went over some of the minor things that players tend to forget. Like positioning on face-offs at various spots around the ice and defensive positioning for the Russian power play. The Russians, we know, set up their power play very deliberately; they will take one minute and fifty-nine seconds of a two-minute penalty to set up one shot if they think they can beat you with that shot. Their power play is no shooting gallery. It is very calculated — and very productive.

After the meeting, one of our defensemen warned me about something he had noticed during the Russian practice this morning. Their forwards seem to shoot the puck as they move outside on the defensemen: rather than try to get around the defensemen and move in for a close shot, they shoot the puck while still in motion to the outside. A good point, thank you. The great majority of NHL players never try such a move.

I'm going to sleep now until five o'clock, then I'm going out for my normal pregame walk, and after that I'll head up to the Forum, fix up a couple of sticks, and get dressed in my usual lazy way. For a normal game in Montreal we warm up at 7:30 P.M., but because of all the pregame pomp and ceremony tonight we'll warm up at 7:15 instead. I doubt that Prime Minister Trudeau will be dropping the puck much before 8:30 P.M.

It's over now. More than one hundred million people watched the game on television in the Soviet Union. Several million watched it in Europe. More than twenty-five million watched it here in Canada and in the United States. And there were almost twenty thousand live witnesses in the Forum. Right now I'll bet that every one of them knows Valery Kharlamov's middle name is Borisovich and Vladislav Tretiak's middle name is Alexandrovich. Everything was set up for a great Canadian party. Then the Russians had to come along and spoil it by playing sixty minutes of hockey better than any of us had dreamed. They beat us 7–3, and they deserved the victory.

I was pretty nervous when we went onto the ice at 7:15 P.M. The Forum was electric; the place was already filled. The fans stood and cheered throughout our workout, and when the Russian players appeared the fans gave them the same welcome. It hit me. My lips became tense. My jaw jutted out. My back stiffened. Determination had settled in. I thought I was ready.

Then came the long list of introductions. Trudeau. Robert Stanfield, the leader of the opposition party. Everyone. The prime minister had called an election the day before, and what a chance to do a little politicking.

We started out quickly; in retrospect, maybe too quickly. Phil Esposito rapped a rebound past Tretiak when the game was only thirty seconds old. I felt pretty confident. Then we scored again. Bobby Clarke clearly won a face-off to Tretiak's right, drew the puck back to Paul Henderson, and he scored. Tretiak never moved on Paul's shot. Two goals in less than seven minutes. We were on our way.

But we were not going to win this game easily. They were on the verge of clicking. They started to pass the puck with beautiful combinations. There was Yevgeny Zimin banging one in from the crease. Goal. 2–1. They received a penalty; they muffled our power play. They got another penalty; they muffled our power play again.

The lull before the storm.

Where oh where was Bobby Orr? They scored again. Boris Mikhailov and Vladimir Petrov broke down ice on a two-on-one, the kind of play the Russians always work on in practice. I stopped Mikhailov's shot — but Petrov put in the rebound. Goal. 2–2.

As I skated to the dressing room, I realized it was going to be a long, tough game, tougher than any of us ever dreamed. Harry came into the room, his tie loosened, perspiration running down his face.

"We're in a hockey game," he said to us. "You didn't expect anything else, did you?" There was an eerie silence in the room. No. No. No. We didn't expect anything else. Of course not. But of course we did. We had superior skills. All we needed to win was a certain amount of effort.

As Harry said it, it sounded as though even he had expected it was going to be easy. For that matter, who hadn't expected us to roll over the Russians?

Valery Kharlamov had not. He was the left wing on the Soviet team's No. 1 line, and he had more moves than Nureyev. He was at the other end of the ice, where he took the puck from Aleksander Maltsev. He skated away from Rod Gilbert. He came around Don Awrey. Suddenly, the puck was between my legs and into the net. Russia led 3–2. And then they began playing keep-away with the puck.

When we did get it, Tretiak was there to take it away. We had a three-on-one. A chance to tie the score. The puck went to Frank Mahovlich. He shot. Tretiak snapped his glove hand over the puck. No goal. Then Gilbert and Jean Ratelle had a two-on-one. Ratelle fed to Gilbert. Tretiak moved out a bit. Save!

The game was half over when Kharlamov came on strong again, breaking through the middle with Maltsev. He started around one of our defensemen. Midway through his move to the outside he fired the puck. I reacted too late — and the puck flew past my glove and into the net. Russia led 4–2.

Our heads were bowed as we skated from the ice at the end of the period, and there was a strange air about the dressing room. We had the monkey off our backs. The Russians had proved over two periods that they were a good hockey team. All Canada would now recognize that. If we lost this game, one game, it would not be a disgrace. Not now! Disgrace — and threats — went out the window. From now on we would be fighting for our hockey lives. Two periods ago we had everything to lose; now we had nothing to lose.

We pressed strongly at the start of the third period, and Clarke eventually scored to pull us within one goal: 4–3. We were physically and emotionally spent, though. The Russians, never letting down, scored three more goals in the last seven minutes of the game. Final score: Russia 7, Team Canada 3. "The catastrophe of the century," was what one NHL executive called it.

September 3

We are back in Toronto, where we had trained; it is almost 4 A.M., and I cannot get to sleep. I keep asking myself all kinds of questions. How did we lose? Why did we lose? What does it all mean now? Questions. Questions. Questions. But few answers. I have to ask myself why I didn't play better.

I think there are a couple of reasons why we lost. We definitely were not in physical or mental shape. We were in shape for practice sessions, intrasquad games and perhaps even early season NHL games against players also not in very good condition. But we were hardly in condition to play against a team of strong skaters who are always in superior shape. Red Berenson was right when he said a few days ago that we were not in shape to play the Russians right now. Further, whenever there is pressure on you to perform well, you tend to become mentally tired. We were a weary team last night.

For some reason we all felt that we had to do everything *now* in order to break the backs of the Russians. The result was that we abandoned our controlled game and began to play scatterbrained hockey. We kept trying to bull our way through three, four, even five Russian players. We became too individualistic. We panicked.

Being down by one or two goals is not a disaster, but we reacted as though the sky had fallen. Then we started to hit, but you must be in shape to hit effectively. We were hitting the Russians all right, but we were bouncing off them.

I hope we learned that you can't intimidate the Russians. They never abandon their style. They are so disciplined, it's amazing. In the end, we started to take cheap shots at them. They took them and laughed at us. From previous experiences I know that when players on one team begin to take cheap shots, the other team thinks they're pretty bush. I can imagine what the Russians think of us now. Here were the frustrated Canadian professionals trying to be vicious. We were very lucky that the referees didn't penalize us more than they did during the last period. Certainly it was not a classy ending.

I'm sure the Russians have a sore-loser feeling about us for another reason: traditionally, at the end of international hockey matches, the players on both sides line up, salute the crowd, and then shake hands with their rivals. Although I was familiar with this tradition, none of us had been informed about it. We don't do it in the NHL. So, at the end of the game, we quickly went to our dressing room while the Russians stayed on the ice, raised their sticks to the crowd, and acted as though they were waiting for us to return for the handshakes. Understandably, they were not pleased when we did not return. Our absence was another ingredient of the sour ending.

Thinking about it, it was a really interesting game. You learn only when you lose. I hope we learned a lot. We obviously did not know what to expect from the Russians, and to a man we did not dream they were as good as they proved to be in Montreal. Everything we heard, everything we saw, led us to believe they were not that good. McLellan and Davidson came back with negative reports from Leningrad. The media and the public were convinced it would be eight straight. With these inputs, we felt mentally confident that there was no way they could beat us. And the early moments of the game followed the expected pattern as we jumped away to our 2–0 lead.

We were heavier by ten to twelve pounds a man, and we were two to three inches taller, but that did not give us any extra leverage in the purely physical battles for the puck; in fact, I suspect the Russians came away with ninety percent of the loose pucks in the first game. Quite a display. Someone described them as twenty Claude Provosts. All bowlegged. True, they don't have beautiful skating strides, like the Ratelles and the Frank Mahovliches, but their short, choppy, muscular strides were quick enough to beat us to the loose pucks and quick enough to stay with us and ahead of us in the backchecking department. Pat Stapleton, who had watched from the stands, also mentioned that he thought their wide-legged stance made them tougher to knock over; we always came out on the worse end of the collisions.

It was quite incredible how they controlled the puck

even in our end, too. Their shooting was not bad, but not great. Except for Kharlamov's twenty-five footer in the second period, all their goals were scored from fairly close in to the net. It is frightening, though that they had an amazing number of scoring chances but refused to shoot the puck, making an extra pass instead. I dare to say that if they had shot the puck just half those times the score probably would have climbed into double figures. Every time I looked there was a Russian player about fifteen feet in front of me with the puck on his stick. Goaltenders don't have much of a chance on shots from that close, but the Russian players kept moving around and waiting for a pass play to develop.

Before the series, all the experts said that Team Canada goaltenders would make the difference, that the Russian goalies were not used to the hard NHL shots and would wilt at the sight and sound of them. Well, it sure did not turn out that way. We never took a real, hard shot at Tretiak from more than twenty-five feet out, because the Russian forwards and defensemen checked us beautifully. Tretiak may have a weakness on long, hard shots, but we never tested him. The only real chances we had against him were rebound shots, and he is extremely agile in close.

The Russians may have a shooting weakness, but they controlled the puck so well in our zone that they set up their players for easy, close-in shots that left the goaltender with little hope of making the save. When you shoot from fifteen feet out, you don't *have* to shoot very hard. Certainly I did not play well, but I don't think I could have stopped more than two of the goals they scored. But two obviously were too many.

Their ability to control the puck was what probably surprised me most about the Russians. I never dreamed they'd be as effective against the NHL players as they were against the National Team players three years ago. Our team went down a lot in attempts to block their shots, but the Russians coolly maneuvered away and skated around the players sprawled on the ice. Shot-blocking is a poor philosophy to use against the Russians: they don't shoot that much, and when they do shoot, their shots are not usually hard enough to warrant the danger of the players taking themselves out of the play in their blocking attempts. Remember, you learn when you lose.

We will have to do a lot of things differently in the second game tomorrow night. We will have to play a controlled, composed game and try to tighten the defense in our own end. I think it is worth mentioning that the best line in the NHL — the Ratelle-Gilbert-Hadfield combination — is basically a passing line and the Russians are basically a passing team. NHL teams tend to have great difficulty stopping a passing line, and Team Canada found it could not stop a passing team either. The Russians have three lines doing what maybe only one of the forty-five lines in the NHL can do.

It is also interesting that the New York line did not play that well against the Russians. They were checked very closely, something that rarely happens to them in the NHL. Perhaps it's because the Russians are more used to defensing such a line — and, as a result, are more effective at it. As a rule, Hadfield is tough and strong in the corners, but he was not too tough or too strong for the Soviet players in the corners. The one NHL line that dominated the Rangers line last year was Boston's Esposito-Cashman-Hodge combination. Hodge, bigger than Hadfield, neutralized him in the corners; Cashman got physical with Gilbert; and Esposito went head-to-head against Ratelle.

I also could not believe the mobility of the Russian

defensemen, whom I had remembered as plodders. Maybe we did not test them enough.

It's all so frustrating. The fans gave me the Bronx cheer when I made an easy save at the end of the game. They took their personal frustrations out on me because I was the last line of resistance. I was the one who let in those seven goals. Maybe I deserved the criticism. I don't know. But it's still difficult to take when you feel badly anyway.

I have to wonder about my goaltending, because I have had practically no success whatsoever in international hockey. It has me thinking. Is my style suited to the international style? I'm a gangling 6 feet 4 inches, so I'm not the quickest goalie in the world with my feet. Maybe the international style demands a mobile goalie. What I'm thinking is that I'll probably never be able to cope with the Russian style of hockey — the quick, crisp passes around the net — unless I change my own goal-tending technique and stay in the net. In the NHL you pretty much have to come out and challenge the shooters. I'll have to think about it some more.

Surprisingly, the Canadian press is not really criticizing us for the 7–3 loss. Not yet, anyway. The writers seem to have a new appreciation for the Russian skills and are emphasizing them rather than our shortcomings. I hope the Canadian people feel the same way.

What effect will this one defeat have on the regular NHL season? Maybe the fans will be turned off at the prospect of watching thirty-nine home games, a great majority of them against expansion teams. I still believe that we have the better players, the better team, and that we will come back and win the series. But what happens if we don't? What will the fans be saying about the million-dollar salaries? Will the owners demand longer training schedules, different training programs? What *will* happen if we lose? Perish the thought.

Sleep.

A fitful sleep, but sleep. And now, at 1 P.M., an empty feeling. Like I have done something wrong, and now I'm waiting around to see what the consequences will be. I don't personally feel that I wronged anyone, but at the same time, when the unexpected happens, there is a helpless feeling. I keep looking around to find signs that this thing has actually happened. Were the events of last night a dream? They seem such a long way away. My memory seems blurred now.

I got up, dressed, and went downstairs to the lobby. Red Fisher of the *Montreal Star* and Ted Blackman of the *Montreal Gazette,* rival sports editors, were there, and they had similar feelings. "It's like something has been taken away from me," Fisher said. I know. I too have lost the feeling that the Canadian professional hockey player, by definition, is superior to all other hockey players in the world. Disillusionment, call it. Now I've got to get it back. We all have to get it back.

We heard some good news, though. James Edmund Park weighed in today at seven pounds, fourteen ounces. Both Gerry and Brad are doing fine. Knowing Emile Francis, he has probably placed one J. E. Park on the New York Rangers' negotiation list. Can you imagine what salaries will be like when J. E. Park gets to be about twenty years old?

After a while, I walked to a nearby greasy spoon for a couple of hamburgers. Bad hamburgers. Terrible hamburgers. Atrocious hamburgers. My stomach ached after the first bite. But the way I felt, filet mignon would have tasted like rawhide. Then I went to practice at Maple

Leaf Gardens. We were all back together again, but it was not the same. The Eight-Straight Gang was one down now and in desperate trouble. I wanted some encouragement. Any encouragement. But I never got it. Maybe I didn't deserve it.

I was really depressed. I spent most of the practice standing alongside the boards, trying my best to act enthused. Tony and E. J. were in goal throughout the practice. They tried me in Game 1. I had failed, and now I was discarded. I am not used to the feeling. Here is the goaltender thought to be the best possible man for the first game, and now he is out in the cold. Very humbling. Very humbling indeed.

Harry and Fergy are going to make eight changes in the lineup for tomorrow night's game, practically a fifty percent change from the opening-game roster. Tony will play goal, and E. J. will be the backup man. I'll be in the stands somewhere. On defense, Park, Bergman and Lapointe will play again, and White, Stapleton and Savard will be added to the roster. The Russians rotated three defense pairs in the first game, while we tried to get by with two pairs and Lapointe in a swingman role. Our guys were exhausted long before the game was over, but their defensemen were fresh. I think we'll be better off rotating six defensemen.

Park and Bergman seem to complement each other pretty well; White and Stapleton have played together for a couple of years in Chicago; and Lapointe and Savard often have worked as a unit in Montreal. Part of the secret of sound defensive play is knowing your partner. You have to know where he wants the puck, on his backhand or his forehand, high or low, and when he wants it. You also must have a pretty good idea when he is likely to take it up ice on a rush so you can stay well back and protect your goaltender.

[56]

Up front, some of Harry's changes were predictable. The Ratelle-Gilbert-Hadfield line will join me in the stands. Mikita will replace Espo at center, on the line with Frank Mahovlich and Cournoyer, and Espo will get Parise and Cashman for his wings. The Clarke-Ellis-Henderson line was our best in Montreal, so it will remain intact. And Bill Goldsworthy will join Peter Mahovlich as a spare forward.

Obviously, we are going to play a different game tomorrow night. Even Harry admitted it. "We've got to get some forecheckers working in the corners," he said. "We can't let the Russians play around with the puck like they did in Montreal." I understand his changes. Mikita is an excellent playmaker, and Frank and Yvan need that type of center. Phil Esposito, on the other hand, does not need great goal-scorers to work with; he needs pluggers in the corners. Cashman and Parise seem ideal for the job.

I also liked something Hadfield said when he found out the Rangers would not be dressing for the second game. "Sure I'm surprised," Vic said, "but this is not the time to gripe. This is the time to pull together."

After the practice, we all had to attend a provincial government reception with the Russian players back at Sutton Place. Like most such functions, it was totally boring. As far as I could see, we were there to sign autographs, to be a presence and mechanically put some lines on scraps of paper. I have mixed emotions about the value of autographs. On the one hand, I can remember collecting them myself, and know there is an emotional contact between the athlete and the fan. On the other hand, I think an autograph should imply more than a mechanical mark, and too often it is only that. This feeling caused me to commit a big blunder at the reception. People kept rushing up and thrusting papers in my face. They honestly think you are duty-bound to sign their pieces of paper. They never say, "Could I please have your autograph?" or "Would you be so kind as to sign this for me?" No. They come at you with blatant shoves, and after a while you get quite aggravated.

This one man raised up his notebook and pointed at it, sort of telling me he wanted my autograph. I said "please" once, then said "please" again. I was really upset. The man said nothing, but I signed anyway. Then he walked away. As he was leaving, I noticed that he was wearing a navy blue blazer with the hammer and sickle crest on his breast pocket. He was a Russian hockey player. I felt like a real jerk. I hope he did not sense my arrogance.

At the reception, all the players were given new Omega wristwatches with thousands of dials and numbers on the face. Mine seems to weigh about thirty pounds. Afterwards, I went upstairs to my room, ordered some pizza that turned out to be even worse than the two hamburgers I had for brunch, and then sat back to watch the Olympics. I played judge with my new watch. In one race I clocked Mark Spitz, the American swimmer, in 51.5 seconds, and his official time was 51.2 something. Not bad. I don't think I'll give the watch back.

September 4

Most Canadian papers do not publish on Sunday, so we all were spared the wrath of the press until this morning. It was funny, really. The editorial columnists gave it to us with both barrels, but the regular hockey writers tried to assess the first game very objectively. They did not muckrake or make scapegoats. No, they simply wrote about how good the Russians were. And they were right.

I really cannot believe Clarence Campbell's comments, though. As the president of the NHL, Clarence automatically commands an audience. When someone asked him what he thought about the first game, he prefaced his remarks with: "I don't want to second-guess and I don't like to second-guess," then came out with a second guess. In the story, he questioned Sinden's decision to play Guy Lapointe and myself and suggested that Harry did it because the game was being played in Montreal.

I think he's being very unfair. Here we are down and defenseless, and he kicks us in the teeth. I really don't think my record in big games or small games is all that bad. I had a good training camp with Team Canada and deserved to play in the first game. I'm burned up about the whole thing.

I'm glad Clarence isn't in my room right now. If he were, I'd probably be as unfair to him as he was to me. I just can't believe he'd say such things.

I see here in another story that Harold Ballard, the owner of the Maple Leafs, says he will give the Russians one million dollars for Valery Kharlamov. Quite a publicity stunt, if you ask me. There's no way Kharlamov would ever leave Russia to play for the Leafs. Ballard knows it; so does everyone else! All Ballard is doing is telling his Toronto fans that the Leafs are trying hard to come up with a winner after all the player defections to the WHA.

Bunny Ahearne, the president of the International Ice Hockey Federation and not a great fan of Canadian professionals, came out with an "I told you so" proclamation from his office in London. "The moral of the story," Ahearne said, "is that you don't have to be a Canadian to be a top-class hockey player." Then he twisted the knife. "I don't think the Canadians will wake up. They're too small-minded. Now they'll start to think up alibis."

Sorry, Bunny, that's the one thing we're not doing, believe me.

Tass, the official Soviet news agency, said simply that the Russian "amateurs" shattered the "myth of the Canadian pros' invincibility."

These comments were mild compared to some of the remarks on the editorial pages of the Toronto papers. The *Star* called it "Hockey Humiliation" and said in a headline that "our team represented us too accurately." "In their world hockey debut," the *Star* said, "our pampered professional darlings played as if they had scarcely been introduced to one another and were outclassed by Russians who earn tiny material rewards by NHL standards. Is it too much to expect that $50,000 to $100,000-a-year hockey players should be in shape in September, like the Russians?" The *Star* went on to criticize our lack of "manners and sportsmanship" during the closing minutes of the game in Montreal. "Team Canada added disgrace to humiliation by taking cheap shots at the Russian players (who responded with admirable self-control) and by failing to stay on the ice for post-game handshakes. It would be idle to deny that there is a tradition in Canadian hockey of trying to assuage the pain of defeat by fouling and fighting opponents. But must our pros act like bush-league soreheads when they skate into the world arena and lose? If we must lose, let it be with some grace."

Whew!

Maybe Jim Coleman's headline in the *Sun* meant the most to us. It read: "Stop blubbering! There's a second game tonight."

But not for me. I practiced this morning with the Black Aces, and tonight I'll be in the stands with them. The Black Aces of a hockey team are the spares. Not utility players — spares! The guys who don't get to play too often. During the practice I thought a lot about Harry's changes for the second game, and now I wonder what good they'll do tonight.

For instance, one advantage of playing in the first game was that we got some live-game conditioning. It was hot in Montreal, and there was a lot of pressure. Somewhere along the line we'll benefit from that. Maybe tonight. In the first game, we presumably went with our best nineteen players, and now we make eight changes. Were we that wrong? Then again, maybe Harry and Fergy saw enough of the Russian style to realize that certain players are better suited to play against them.

Finally, when you lose a game and play the same team again right away, you usually show up for the second match with a fierce desire to get even. Now maybe only half the team will feel that way. I don't envy Sinden and Ferguson, that's for sure. What a tough decision. I will say that based on our performance the other night most of the benched players don't deserve to dress tonight.

As expected, the Black Aces were flat at practice. Disappointed, down, depressed. None of us is used to watching a game from the seats. To make things worse, one of Hadfield's shots hit my injured finger and now it hurts like crazy again. It had not bothered me in the game at Montreal.

After the workout, Harry and Fergy took us to see a horror movie. A full-length video-tape replay of the Montreal disaster. Right there in living color. We all watched with our heads in our hands and our mouths open. It was torture.

It's hard to believe how many times the Russians beat us to loose pucks and how many times they had two-on-one breaks and how many times they got off shots on the one-on-one plays that usually prove harmless in the

NHL. Someone counted ten one-on-ones when the Russians beat us cleanly at the defense.

In the NHL, defensemen usually break up the one-on-one very easily by taking out the shooter with a body check before he shoots. I don't understand how the Russians did it. I mean, I don't think their stickhandling is that great. Sure, a Kharlamov and a Maltsev are superior stickhandlers, and they do use their feet well. But maybe it's the way they delude you. They pass the puck so well that maybe the defenseman is worried more about a possible pass than a shot on goal.

I think I learned something myself from the horror movie. During action around the net, the Russian forwards positioned themselves to the side of the net, right off the goalposts, almost along the extension of the goal line. NHL players, as a rule, tend to congregate in front of the net. I'm used to kicking rebounds out towards the corners, away from NHL forwards, but in the first game I directed rebounds right onto the sticks of the Russian forwards. Better remember that the next time I play.

On one play, it looked as though I made a great save on Zimin right at the goal mouth. I did make some saves, but this was not one of them. What looked like a great save was actually an intercepted pass. Someone had passed the puck across the goal mouth to Zimin, who was wide open at the edge of the crease. Cournoyer or Mahovlich or Esposito would have tried to flip the puck over me in a flash. Not Zimin. I slid across the goal mouth in a desperate attempt to block the shot, with my stick hand out in front. The puck came across, hit my glove, and stayed under me. Great save? No. Zimin had tried to pass the puck back across to Aleksander Yakushev, who was standing all alone at the other side of the crease and undoubtedly would have scored an easy goal into an open net. You rarely, if ever, see such close-in

Goaltending has its ups — I'm leaping to deflect one of
Boris Mikhailov's (13) shots.

pass plays in the NHL. The players always shoot the puck first.

Later in the day I talked with Rick Noonan again, and he told me the Russians have really changed their approach. In the old days under Anatoli Tarasov, the great coach whom many consider to be the "Father of Soviet Hockey," the Russians always had long, hard, serious, glum practices. Under Vsevolod Bobrov, the new coach, the Russians seem to fool around more on the ice. One of the Soviet trainers told Rick before the first game that losing the series would not be the end of the world for the Russian players. He said they expected to lose three games in Canada and get one tie. Anything else would be gravy. Rick also said that on the plane from Montreal to Toronto after the first game one of the Russian players told him that "it took us about ten minutes of the game to realize the Canadian professionals are ordinary human beings like us."

I'm afraid, though, that this series will be analyzed and analyzed ad nauseam. People in the street. Cab drivers. Bellboys. Waiters. Writers. Coaches. League presidents. Prime ministers. Everyone. They all have a theory. They all picture themselves as a coach or a player, and they become theoretical and hypothetical. It's so much bull, believe me. They're all sitting there and playing verbal games to make themselves sound important. We have to play the real games. We know what we have to do. Or do we?

I never realized how bad life with the Black Aces would be. We have to sit in the stands, and we also have to attend all the functions that government officials throw every day or so. Today it was another federal banquet. I can't tolerate these affairs anymore; they smack of politics in the worst sense.

Now the politicians are saying that this series will promote a closer understanding between peoples of different nations with different life styles and will foster a spirit of brotherhood and closer attachment. In some remote way the politicians may be right, but there are a lot of barriers to a world of understanding and brotherhood and I don't know whether a hockey series, especially one which has been approached like this one, will have any significant benefit. What I mean to say is, as far as the vast majority of Canadians are concerned, this series was not conceived in the spirit of brotherhood and understanding but as a means of putting down the Russians and reasserting our claim to world hockey supremacy.

It is little wonder that the public rarely takes politicians' remarks seriously. It is difficult to accept statements that the speaker and his audience both view as being so much gibberish. But apparently that's politics and diplomacy. Great!

The banquet did give me a chance to use my stopwatch again. Each time a politician got up to speak, I timed his stay at the microphone. Mitchell Sharp, the Canadian minister for external affairs, won the gold medal. He also tried to be funny in his speech. He talked for the longest time about Canadian hospitality, then apologized to the Russians for the lack of it at the end of the game in Montreal. "Of course," he said, "our players were too hospitable during the game." I did not laugh. The Russian Black Aces were lucky. They did not have to attend the reception, probably because they had been warned there would be a demonstration nearby protesting the treatment of Soviet Jews inside Russia.

Sinden and Ferguson are making two technical changes in our plan for the second game. First of all, we will fire the puck into the Russian zone all night and then chase it with some strong, vigorous forechecking. This is a good idea because in the first game we played too much for the pass at the blue line, and we simply are not a good passing team. The Russians broke up our passes fairly easily with some strong backchecking by their forwards and some aggressive play by their defensemen at the blue line. They took the puck from us, and moved quickly the other way on a three-on-two or two-on-one break. Tonight we'll throw the puck into their end and try to take it away from them. I'm certain we will force them into mistakes if we can apply constant forechecking pressure.

Second, instead of having our wings check the Russian defensemen in our zone, they will stay in our corners a bit longer to give the defensemen some extra help. The Russians use their defensemen as pivots on the attack with their forwards making most of the plays and taking most of the shots, so our centers will try to handle the two defensemen alone.

As I mentioned yesterday, we will be skating three defensive units, not two, but I don't think we will rotate our lines and defenses in strict five-man units, the way the Russians do. Each time the Russians change lines they send five men over the boards. We'll probably still change our lines and defenses separately.

All the changes worked very well, and we won 4–1. Tony Esposito played a strong, confident game in goal and repeatedly made the big saves. The defensemen all stayed up, kept the Russian forwards away from the net, and managed to get the puck out of our zone without any great difficulty. And up front, we charged into the corners all night, particularly Cashman and Parise, and at times intimidated the Russians — something I thought impossible. It was very blatant at times. A lot of high sticks were rubbed under the noses of the Russians to suggest what might happen later. There were also a few cheap shots. Sometimes it was almost uncomfortable and embarrassing to watch. If I had been one of the Russian players, I'd have thought: "These Canadians must be awfully brutal to be going around and doing these things all the time."

Cashman was very effective as he worked overtime in the corners to clear the Russians away from the puck and get it out to Phil Esposito. It was Cash's persistence that led directly to our first goal as Esposito took a pass-out and from his favorite spot in the slot about twenty feet in front of the net whipped the puck past Tretiak.

We scored again early in the third period when Cournoyer took a perfect pass from Park and beat Tretiak on a breakaway, but the Russians closed the score to 2–1 as Yakushev scored on a power play. Despite all the recognition Kharlamov is getting, Yakushev may be just as good. He is 6 feet 3 inches, weighs 205 pounds, plays left wing, and skates like a combination of Bobby Orr and Frank Mahovlich. Some of the writers are even calling him the "Poor Man's Frank Mahovlich."

Shortly after Yakushev scored, Pat Stapleton went off for hooking, and suddenly a pall fell over the Gardens, in expectation of the tying goal! Peter Mahovlich and Phil Esposito were out killing the penalty, and then Peter got control of the puck at center ice.

When Peter gets his 6-foot 5-inch body in motion, he can confuse you. Even embarrass you. Anyway, he left a couple of Russian defensemen wondering where he went, moved in on Tretiak, gave him a half-dozen double fakes, and then slid a backhander into the open net. Brother Frank scored a couple of minutes later, so it was a big night for the Espositos from Sault Sainte Marie and the Mahovliches from Schumacher.

After the game we remained on the ice to shake hands with the Russians and then departed to a standing ovation from the crowd. While we were celebrating the victory, the Russians were on the other side of the Gardens complaining about the officiating. Complaining? Andrei Starovoitov, the head of the Soviet Hockey Federation, actually tried to kick down the door to the referees' dressing room.

"The American referees," Starovoitov steamed, "let the Canadian players perform like a bunch of barbarians."

September 5

Headline in the *Toronto Sun:* WE DID IT! 4–1. No editorials today. No muckraking. Just stories about how *we* won the game.

There is no doubt in my mind that Tony will play again in Winnipeg tomorrow night. He deserves to play. So I'm still out in the woods, or still in the stands. It hurts a bit, and it will continue to hurt. I have not had the feeling very often in my athletic career, but I will learn from it. At least I hope I will.

A funny thing happened on the ice before practice. Dennis Hull was at one blue line and Marcel Dionne was at the other. Then they both skated toward the face-off circle at center ice. Dionne handed Hull a Soviet pennant, and Hull tapped Marcel lightly on the knees with the blade of his stick. They then shook hands, smiled, and nodded their heads. How's that for a little spirit of understanding between people?

After practice, I met my brother Dave, who plays goal

for the Buffalo Sabres, for lunch in Yorkville. We sat around for a couple of hours and talked about goaltending theories and styles, something you normally never talk about. For instance, I like to stand up and go out to challenge the shooters. Tony Esposito, on the other hand, prefers to flop down with his legs spread toward the posts, and he stays in his net almost all the time.

Dave and I both agreed that Tony's style is more suited for beating the Russians. You must play more in the net to contain the slick, close-in passing game the Russians work so perfectly. The advantage to going out to cut down an angle on the shooter is that you presumably force him into a position where his only option is to shoot the puck at an almost invisible target. The more you go out at the shooter, the less the shooter sees of the net.

But the Russians are not simply shooters. They are also passers. When I leave my net to cut down the angle, they hold their shot and then pass off to a teammate. Suddenly there is a new shooter with a new angle, and I am caught well out of position. The more you do go out to cut down the angle the more you must move when and if the original shooter decides to pass the puck instead. But for someone like Tony, who stays in the net most of the time, this is much less of a problem. Still, you also must stop the shot.

One of the most important theories of goaltending is that the shooter must beat you. You try to get as much of your body in front of the puck as possible, so that you *force* the shooter to beat you, the entire you, not just an arm or a leg. You never want to give him the easy chance to flip the puck into an open net. Well, with my style — a technique, mind you, that has been pretty effective in the NHL shooting galleries — I seem to give the Russians these easy, close-in opportunities for unobstructed goals.

As I mentioned, the Russians play their forwards off to the corners of the posts, not in front of the net. They like to have their forwards break from the corners and either tip in a goal-mouth pass or smack in a rebound. When someone is off to your side, it's almost impossible to see him because of the lack of total peripheral vision. Then a shot comes towards you. It's wide. Or is it? It may be a pass to the winger cutting in.

So, it seems to me, and Dave agrees, that the best way to play against the Soviets is to remain in the net. Concede the shooters their shots from twenty-five and thirty feet. Expect the pass instead, and think about the wingers coming at you from the corners. In this regard both Tony and E. J. have styles that are more compatible with the way the Russians play. Tony stays in the net, while E. J. basically remains at the top part of the crease and simply turns his body in the direction of the action.

Dave told me that he had made some measurements last year to find out just how much of the net a goaltender blocks off when he goes out to cut down the shooter's angle. He found that for every foot a goalie moves out, he cuts off only three-fourths of an inch of the net when the shooter is at the blue line, which does not make the effort worthwhile. In fact, the physical benefit may be zero, though there is certainly a psychological advantage for the goaltender because the shooter thinks he sees much less of the net. Possibly the shooter feels defeated when the goaltender moves out towards him. It's all very intriguing.

I've been thinking about it for a few days now, however, and I'm definitely going to change my style. I'm going to stay in my net, like Tony and E. J. I'm big, of course, and I hardly have great mobility or great lateral movement. But because I'm big I also should be able to cut down enough of the shooter's angle by remaining near the net. For instance, it stands to reason that if 5-foot 7-inch, 160-pound Rogatien Vachon and 6-foot, 4-inch, 210 pound Ken Dryden take similar stances in the goal, then Dryden will block more of it. So there will be a new Dryden in the goal from now on. I hope it will be a new Dryden, anyway.

Dave and I also talked about what effect the series might have on the NHL. Dave hoped the coaches of the poorer teams in the NHL were watching the Russians and learning something from them. The Russian team has both a number of talented players and a number of players without great talent. They play unbelievably well as a unit by using three separate five-man combinations through the game. These five men know one another like brothers.

Now why shouldn't some of the weaker NHL teams adopt such tactics? Not only don't they have individual stars, but they don't play cohesively either, so they miss the play-offs. Maybe the Russian system would be the difference between winning and losing. But I'm afraid that NHL teams would not be willing to discipline themselves sufficiently to make such a system work. What kind of motivation is there for such discipline? Score twenty goals in the NHL and you get a big raise no matter where your team finishes.

Later, I asked some NHL people how many of their teams had coaches, scouts or general managers at the first two games of the series. Would you believe that of the six teams that missed the play-offs last year only two sent people to Montreal or Toronto? I don't understand it. Here's a chance to learn something new, and they're not interested.

I have to laugh at something I read about the subject of the NHL changing over to the unit system employed by the Russians. Someone suggested that it is a pretty sensible way to play because it does provide a definite amount of on-ice cohesion. "Yes," an NHL executive said, "it's not a bad idea." Then another NHL type said that by playing units, stars like Bobby Orr and Brad Park would appear only every three shifts instead of every other change. "Yeah, you're right," the first NHL guy said. "The unit system is a lousy idea." I guess it depends on how many defensemen you have of approximately equal ability.

Talking with Dave for a few hours soothed my depression, and I was in a good mental state when we arrived in Winnipeg about 8 P.M. I spent most of the 1969–70 season here playing for the National Team until it disbanded and attending law school at the University of Manitoba. I did not enjoy my year here, though it was not the city's fault; for one thing, I had a fiancée, now my wife, in Ithaca, N.Y.; for another, I did not play well.

I remember vividly that Winnipeg adopted the National Team but gave it little support until the team folded at New Year's. Then suddenly the city embraced the Nationals and led an outcry against the decision to disband the team. As far as Winnipeg was concerned, it was another low blow struck by the powerful Eastern establishment. It did not matter to it that the rest of Canada agreed with the decision to break up the team when the International Ice Hockey Federation decreed that the Nationals could not use nine professionals in the World Tournament. Winnipeg saw the team's demise as a shafting by the effete Easterners and that was that.

Quite understandably, the West has a definite inferiority complex. The East tends to dump on the West because, well, Easterners are more advanced socially and intellectually (they think!). To make things worse, they have most of the head offices of the major corporations and control the flow of most of Canada's money.

It was ironic, though, that the only games that ever sold out in the Winnipeg Arena were exhibitions against the Russians. We could not sell out for the Czechs, for instance, and when strong professional teams like the Omaha Knights and the Montreal Voyageurs came to town we were lucky to attract three thousand people. Yet there was a great outcry about losing "our" National Team.

Winnipeg has always felt that the NHL should have included the city in its expansion plans. When it finally got a franchise with a major-league label, the Winnipeg Jets of the World Hockey Association, it pulled the big coup of signing Bobby Hull of the Chicago Black Hawks and the NHL for three million dollars. And what happened? Just when Winnipeg thought it was major league, the NHL slapped its face once again and refused to let Hull play for Team Canada. According to everyone in Winnipeg we are not really Team Canada but Team NHL. Winnipeg's attitude is understandable, and largely justified, but unfortunate. In one sense we are, but it is really a matter of semantics.

September 6

At 12:30 A.M. Andrei Starovoitov and Vsevolod Bobrov placed a phone call to Harry Sinden and John Ferguson. They were still upset about the officiating in the Toronto game and demanded that Sinden and Ferguson not select the same referees — Steve Dowling and Frank Larsen of the United States — for the fourth game of the series in Vancouver. According to a preseries agreement, the Russians would select the officials for Games 1, 3, 6 and 8, while we would select them for Games 2, 4, 5 and 7. The Russians made it quite clear that they wanted the first-game referees — Len Gagnon and Gordie Lee, also of the United States — to officiate the next two games.

Harry and Fergy had no complaints about the work of Gagnon and Lee in Game 1, so rather than make an international incident out of what seemed like a reasonable protest to the Russians, they agreed to pick Gagnon and Lee for the fourth game in Vancouver. "Sometime we'll ask the Russians to reciprocate in some way," Harry said.

The Black Aces' status was very clear when we showed up for practice at the Arena. There were two dressing rooms: a large one for the regulars, a closet for the Aces. The regulars got two towels each; the Aces got one. The regulars seemed to have an unlimited supply of Cokes in their cooler; we had to go into their room to steal one. The lines of distinction had been drawn. Before we felt we were on the edge, now we were out in the cold.

While dressing for the morning practice, I couldn't find one of my goalie's skates. I looked in my equipment bag, under the bench, all over the room. Finally I noticed that my skate was being used as a stop to keep our door open. The blade was wedged between the bottom of the door and the floor. Red Berenson also noticed the skate and said, "Well, Dryden, that's the first thing you've stopped all week." Thanks!

At practice we were the odd men out, and it was hard to take. During training camp we all felt we would play a certain amount during the games. We were, of course, under the assumption that things would go well, that we would win eight straight. Now we realized how difficult the series was going to be and that Harry and Fergy would have to go with the best lineup every night. There were some grumblings and some complaints in the closet-sized room of the Black Aces. Such things come naturally at times like this, but I never think seriously about them.

The Arena was jammed. SRO, with the Russian Black Aces seated in the first row directly behind our bench. Just before the game started, though, Alan Eagleson whom Red Fisher of the *Montreal Star* calls "The Godfather," made the Russians an offer they couldn't refuse. He gave them some of Harold Ballard's seats at the other side of the rink and demanded that they move. Pronto! The Russians did not like it. "We're not cattle," one of their interpreters said. "If you don't move the game won't start," Eagleson said. They moved.

Our game plan was the same as in Toronto: shoot the puck into the corners and muscle it away from the Russians. Bobrov made some changes in the Soviet lineup. He benched five regulars and introduced his Kid Line — Molodov Troika, I think they call it — of Vyacheslav Mikhailovich Anisin, Aleksander Ivanovich Bodunov and Yuri Vasilyevich Lebedev. "We want them to learn," Bobrov said.

At the start, at least, we controlled the flow of play. Early on, Parise barged through a pack of Russians to rap in a rebound of Bill White's shot. Then the Soviets got a penalty. We tried to press. Petrov intercepted a pass. A shorthanded goal for the Soviets. But we continued to hit, with Bergman and Ron Ellis knocking the Russians all over the ice. Late in the first period Ratelle, back in the lineup but without his usual New York linemates, scored to give us a 2–1 lead.

In the second period Cashman dug the puck from a corner and fed it out to Espo for one of his patented goals to make it 3–1. And then another Canadian power play. Oops! Another shorthanded goal for the Russians! This time Kharlamov floated around center ice as our point men stayed up at the blue line. Suddenly Gennady Tsygankov, a Russian defenseman, got control of the puck in the corner to Tretiak's right. He fired it across the ice off the far boards and into center ice, and there was Kharlamov with a breakaway. The Russians now had scored three shorthanded goals in the series, and we had yet to score on our power play. No doubt about it, we really miss Bobby Orr on the power play, and at a lot of other times.

Kharlamov's goal did not deflate us, though, because Henderson promptly regained the two-goal advantage with a very pretty off-balance shot after taking a pass from Ron Ellis. So we led 4–2. But suddenly things changed. The Russians began to set the tempo of play and it looked as though they'd score any minute. They did. First it was Lebedev, deflecting a shot past Tony to make the score 4–3, and then it was Bodunov, beating Tony from the crease after a perfect pass-out from the corner.

Tony Esposito played very well. With thirteen seconds left in the game he preserved the tie with a great save on Aleksander Maltsev. Tretiak kept the Russians in the game with thirty-eight saves, including a point-blank grab of a Henderson shot from about eight feet out in the final period. "That kid," Sinden said later, "was not supposed to have a glove hand." Final score: 4–4.

Later we tried to rationalize the result by saying we blew a certain victory. We didn't blow it. The Russians took it. We said they were lucky and got all the breaks. No way. They were behind, but they didn't get discouraged and they made their own breaks. They showed they can play at least two kinds of game. In Montreal they applied sustained pressure for sixty minutes. Here in Winnipeg they were smug opportunists. It must be comforting for them to realize that they are never out of a game. How often do teams come back twice from two goals down in the NHL?

For the second time in three games Tretiak was selected as his team's "Star of the Game," and now he has won two rings. Bobrov turned comedian when someone asked him what Tretiak planned to do with them. He smiled and said, "He will give one to his new wife, I suppose, and he'll probably give the other to one of his old girl friends."

The Russian kids really impressed me tonight. They obviously are the products of the modern Soviet hockey system because they shoot harder and more often than their older teammates. They also seem to be more accustomed to rough play.

September 7

I spent most of the morning talking to some former National Team players who live around Winnipeg. Most of them have mixed feelings about Canada's troubles in this series. For years they were insulted because of their constant losses to the Russians, and now they feel vindicated. I can't really blame them.

Clarence Campbell is also staying at our hotel here. I was still pretty upset over the comments he made the other day, so I went upstairs to his room, knocked on the door, and had a friendly chat with him. I told him how upset I was; how I thought what he had said was a cheap second guess, and how I thought he had been totally unfair. To say the least, he seemed surprised that I was upset. But I think he pretty much agreed with what I told him, because he said that what appeared in print had been taken out of context. He also said he had been misquoted but had long since learned not to yell

Vladislav Tretiak is down, but not quickly enough to stop Peter Mahovlich in the second game at Toronto.

I had my troubles in the first game in Montreal.

"I've been misquoted" because no one believes it. I understand what he said to me and feel better.

The "Dissension on Team Canada" stories have hit the papers. Dan Proudfoot, one of the writers who rode on our bus from practice yesterday, suggested in the *Toronto Globe and Mail* that Vic Hadfield and Rick Martin had to be talked out of quitting the team. I don't know, but I think the article is quite unfair. I'm sure Hadfield and Martin, like the rest of us, are aware that Harry and Fergy have been using the players they think are best in every game and any words of protest are the natural discontented grumblings, rather than veiled threats. Hadfield scored on me during practice in Winnipeg and I said to him, "Geez Murphy, I thought you were back in Toronto." He laughed.

Cashman was the hit of the workout. First of all he offered one of the Russian players a cup of soup. Then he went back into the dressing room, lathered his face with shaving cream, returned to the ice, and promptly made two all-out rushes from sideboard to sideboard as the Russian players looked on in bewilderment and we just laughed. "Look, guys, still moist," Cash yelled as he squished his fingers through the shaving cream, just like Bobby Hull does in the commercial.

Harry took me aside after the workout and told me that I would be starting in Vancouver. Later on, I was late as usual for the bus to the airport. What happened today was that I forgot to pack a book into my suitcase and remembered it after I had checked out of the hotel. So I went upstairs to get it, and when I finally walked onto the bus the guys gave me the Bronx cheer. In college, being fifteen minutes late meant you were fifteen minutes early. In the NHL, though, fifteen minutes late means you're thirty minutes late. I think I'll set my watch fifteen minutes ahead from now on. If I remember.

Before the flight out to Vancouver, I bought the *Winnipeg Tribune*. There, on page one, above the fold, was a bold headline: THE BIG, FAT NHL HAS LOST ITS PATENT ON THE GAME OF HOCKEY. Jack Matheson, the *Tribune*'s sports editor, outdid himself in this story. It's too bad. He's a good writer, but he gets so involved in his anti-NHL feelings that it oftentimes poisons his writing. This was a real World Hockey Association propaganda diatribe. He wrote, "If this is Team Canada, I want no part of it. It's Team NHL, and we've all been sucked into a monstrous trap. We have sundry things to be proud about in this country, but the NHL isn't one of them."

Among other things, he attacked the NHL because there was only a thirty-second moment of silence before the game last night for the Israeli Olympians who were killed at Munich. Calling it the most outrageous insult of all, Matheson wrote, "Thirty seconds was the best the NHL could do because there were television commitments and a guy has to make a buck." I think he is overreaching there.

Let's face it: you can make an argument to support a premise that the NHL has lost its patent on the game. Obviously. And certainly you can criticize many aspects of the NHL's daily operation. However, you lose your credibility on that point by branching off into a series of critical remarks against the NHL that are strictly cheap shots and have no relationship to what you are trying to prove.

On the flight to Vancouver, I had a chance to think about some things that Douglas Fisher was talking about a few days ago. He is a former member of Parliament who writes a political column now and is a member of the board of Hockey Canada. Lamenting the lack of coaching throughout the Canadian hockey system, Fisher said. "What NHL coaches get by on, in part, is their ability to be psychers. That's where you get all this talk: are they up for the game or are they down?" On the whole I have to agree with Fisher. There is very little coaching done at the NHL level. The coaches simply try to get you ready for the next game. We prepare for one game, not a game six months from now or even next week.

Fisher also bemoaned the dominance of the NHL in Canadian hockey. "The amount of organized play in Canada betwen eight and fourteen years of age," he said, "amounts to a virtual industry, but by the time the kid is sixteen organization drops to a trickle. We have crystallized a kind of toy game that we want our kids to play: you either make it by sixteen or you're through. What we really need is a game that can be played by the majority of people until they are twenty-five or thirty." He used Phil Esposito as an example. "Esposito could have been a hockey dropout," Fisher said. "He is the best individual player in this series, yet when he was a kid he was passed by because he was an ugly duckling."

Again I must agree with Fisher's reasoning. A Canadian boy really has to show something by the age of seventeen or eighteen or else he's through with organized hockey. He has to show he's Junior-A material and therefore potential NHL material by that time. He must be big. He must have a good shot. But look what is happening in the United States. The colleges have proved that players still have pro potential as late as twenty-two or twenty-three. Maybe you don't have to play sixty or seventy games a year when you are seventeen and eighteen, as we think in Canada. Maybe you could play just thirty-five or so games and also go to school. Unfortunately, there isn't a reasonable chance to do both in Canada at this time. Now, perhaps, there will be an increased tolerance for other ways, new ways that can be effective if given the chance.

Once in Vancouver we went directly to the Bay Shore Inn, but we missed Howard Hughes, unfortunately. He had checked out earlier in the week and flown to Managua, Nicaragua. Or so they told us. At least we can use all the elevators. Gary Bergman, Brad Park, Bill White and I went to Hy's Steak House for, naturally, steaks, and when we returned to the hotel bad news awaited us.

At practice back in Winnipeg this morning one of Red Berenson's shots hit Serge Savard on the right ankle. Serge limped off the ice. On the plane his ankle began to swell up and Joe Sgro, the trainer, had to wrap it with ice packs. Serge went for X rays when we landed here, and now the doctors say his ankle is cracked. Poor Serge.

As a junior amateur he had had a couple of knee operations. Then three years ago he crashed into a goalpost at the Montreal Forum and shattered his left leg. Two years ago he broke the same leg in the same place and the doctors had to graft bone from his right hip to the broken bones on his left leg. Last year he returned to the Canadiens' lineup in February but a month later was back in the hospital. A fire broke out in the St. Louis hotel where we were staying after a game against the Blues, and a number of hotel guests were trapped in their rooms. Savard and several other Montreal players helped with the rescue by climbing ladders and kicking open windows of the smoke-filled rooms. Well, in kicking open a window Serge cut open his right ankle and the doctors spent hours trying to extract chips of glass from the wound. He could not play for about ten days after that injury.

Now here he is just skating himself back into top condition and the ankle gets broken again. Serge really played well in both Toronto and Winnipeg after sitting out the game in Montreal. He'll be returning to Montreal tomorrow so the Canadiens' team doctors can inspect the ankle themselves.

[83]

September 8

Team Canada, as I said before, has a great nonrule: goalies don't have to wear full gear during the game-day skate in the morning. I don't think there's a goaltender alive who does not imagine himself as a seventy-five-goal scorer playing left wing. I remember playing a game in Thompson, Manitoba, a few years ago, right after the National Team folded. We beat this intermediate amateur team about 18–2 the first night, and after we rolled up about a 15–1 lead in the second period the next night I convinced our coach to let me play forward during the third period. Suddenly I was Mahovlich and Howe and Gilbert and Esposito and Beliveau. I scored a goal and two assists in the third period, and, in fact, I still have the puck from the goal. Are you listening, Scotty Bowman? Without a doubt it is one of the proudest moments of my hockey career.

The Vancouver papers are suggesting that Sinden's decision to play me tonight is a mistake, considering that Tony played so well in the last two games. On the other hand, it could be a brilliant decision, considering that I now have something to prove to Harry, to Fergy, my teammates, the Russian players and everyone else. I remember the last game I played against the Russians here three years ago. It was my first game against them, and they poured nine goals past me. I had to make one of my better saves with ten seconds to go — turning away a deflection — to keep the score from mounting into double figures. I was never so tired after a game. They fired forty-five shots at me, not an incredible amount by NHL standards but an indoor record for the Russians. As I've said, the Russians rarely shoot until they have the perfect shot. That night they had forty-five perfect shots. And I'm not just trying to defend my reputation, either. I felt like the ball in a pinball machine. All night long I got ready for a shot, moved, went down, got up, got ready, moved, went down, got up, got ready, moved — and then fished the puck from the net. Once I got so frustrated that I yelled out, "Damn it, shoot the thing."

I remember one other thing about that game. Maltsev, a classic center in that he is a superb playmaker and puckhandler, also played for the Soviet team then, and after the Russians had scored five or six goals he skated past the goal and winked at me. He wasn't being sarcastic. No, it was a good-natured wink. I'll never forget it.

At the morning meeting Harry said he was switching back to five defensemen instead of six. The five defensemen he named weren't too happy — you really need six defensemen in these games — and they told Harry about it. He agreed with them, and now Bill White has been restored to the lineup.

It's difficult not to think about what Tretiak has been doing to us. In fact, we seem to think and talk about him more than any of the other Soviet players. Like what Eddie Johnston was saying this afternoon. "Pressure doesn't seem to bother him at all," E. J. said. "I don't think he's superhuman. Eventually it will get to him. He's young now. He'll learn what pressure is, but you look at him out there and if he gets a bad goal scored on him, well, it doesn't seem to bother him. But that's only part of it. How many rebounds has he given up? He stands there, traps the puck in his pads, and people wait around for it to fall, but nothing happens.

"How would he do in the NHL? Let's just say he's doing pretty well against the best in the NHL right now.

I thought — and I'm not alone — that when some of our big guys started shooting at him he'd be looking for the door to his dressing room. I thought our guys would run right over him. Geez, he's only twenty, and he's doing this to us."

Well, he did it again. It was 5–3 this time. All I remember are the boos. It's hard to say that a team feels defeated before the game, but, well, we seemed to have a sort of a "let's get it over with and get to Moscow" attitude about things in the dressing room. The Russians jumped to a quick 2–0 lead, scoring identical power-play goals in the first eight minutes while Bill Goldsworthy was in the penalty box both times. On both goals, Petrov had the puck to my left, then slid it back to Vladimir Lutchenko at the blue line. Lutchenko looked around, waited for his forwards to get into position, and then fired towards the net. The first time, Boris Mikhailov deflected Lutchenko's shot through my legs; the second time, he tipped it into the corner. I hardly had a chance on either goal.

Then we settled down, and early in the second period Gilbert Perreault banked a pass-out off one of the Russian defensemen and past Tretiak to close the score 2–1. Suddenly, though, I became very shaky. Someone took a harmless shot from about twenty feet; I caught it easily and brought it down with my hand. Or at least I thought I had, but the puck was behind me, rolling towards the empty net. Fortunately Don Awrey was there to slide the puck back under me. A few seconds later I juggled another easy shot from about forty feet. My shakiness didn't cost us any goals, but it certainly did not inspire my teammates.

Then Yuri Blinov beat me on a two-on-one, and a few minutes later Vladimir Vikulov scored from in close, and suddenly we were down 4–1. For all practical purposes, we were out of the game. The fans in Vancouver booed like crazy. At one end of the ice Tretiak was making unbelievable saves, and at the other end of the ice Shaky Dryden was not. Well, I think the Russian goals were good goals. Sure, I didn't look good making some saves because I was shaky, but I don't think I could have stopped any of their goals.

After the game Phil Esposito was interviewed live on national television and blasted the Canadian fans, the Canadian press and everyone else for their treatment of Team Canada's players. "We're trying our best and giving it our all," Espo said, "and I wish the hell you people would realize that. These Russians are great hockey players. Why not give them credit and stop blaming us?"

In the dressing room we all were downcast. The Russians led the series now 2–1–1 and the next four games would be in Moscow. Frank Mahovlich was stunned by it all. "I'm ready to believe anything now," Frank said. "After seeing what the Russians did to us at our game here in Canada, I'm afraid nothing in sports is sacred anymore. If someone gives them a football they'll beat the Dallas Cowboys and win the Super Bowl in two years."

September 9

It is 12:15 A.M., and I'm leaving right now for Montreal. But I can't get away from Tretiak and Yakushev and Kharlamov and Mikhailov and their friends. They're on the same flight. I'll bet it will be a longer flight for me, though.

As the engines drone on, Gary Bergman, Bill White

and Rick Martin are playing card tricks. The Russians are in a different cabin, separated from us. The one bad thing about this series — besides our losses, of course — is the language barrier between the two teams. None of our players can speak Russian, and none of their players can speak English. So we cannot converse with one another. It's really frustrating.

The Russians obviously are interesting guys. It would be great to talk hockey with them. Talk about anything. But there is no way. I'd like to ask them what they think of Canadian professional hockey players. Are they impressed with us or not impressed? And in what ways? Sadly, there is no way for me to find out. Press conferences only produce diplomatic responses, the type interpreters have memorized. So I learn nothing. Here are guys for whom we have a newfound respect; now they are sitting only twenty yards away, and we can't even talk to them, although we communicate a bit by hand signals. Sort of thumbs up or thumbs down.

I sat for a while with Aggie Kukolowicz, a former NHL player who is now with Air Canada and was for years the airline's representative in Moscow. Aggie used to skate with the Russian players, and he always told them how good the Canadian pros were and how they could beat the Russians without much effort. I asked him what he would say to his Russian friends in Moscow about our poor performance in the first four games. He said he'd mention some of our mistakes: the lack of conditioning, the time of year, the obvious overconfidence. But he did not think they'd accept these excuses. Aggie speaks Russian fluently, and he spends most of his day with the Russian players. But he really doesn't seem to know much more about them than the rest of us.

I'd really like to talk with Vyacheslav Starshinov, one of the oldest Soviet players, who now is nearing retirement after a brilliant international career. Starshinov is pursuing his doctorate at the Institute of Sports and Physical Culture in Moscow, and as part of his thesis he brought a questionnaire to Canada and asked us to fill it out. It was thorough and interesting. Among other things, Starshinov asked if the athlete in a Canadian society lives by the moral standards of that society or by his own standards. He also asked what an athlete thinks his responsibilities to society are.

Right now I'd like to take a cram Berlitz course in modern Russian. All I know how to say is *spassiba*. Thank you.

For part of the flight I also chatted with Warren Reynolds, a former basketball player for the Canadian Olympic team. Warren had watched some of the hockey games, and he compared the Russians' hockey style with their basketball style. In basketball, Reynolds said, the Russians work all their plays off picks and weaves. In hockey they do much the same thing. In fact, by NHL standards they are guilty of an incredible number of interference penalties. Warren also pointed out that the Russians always try for the high-percentage, close-in lay-up shot in basketball; indeed, they rarely shoot jump shots or any other shots from more than ten or fifteen feet away. Their style is the same in hockey. When you think of it, except that one game is played on ice and the other on wood, there is not a whole lot of difference between hockey and basketball strategy.

We finally landed in Montreal at 10:30 in the morning and Jocelyn Guevremont drove me to my apartment. Three minutes later I was asleep. When I woke up at about 1:30 P.M., I could not open my eyes. I had left my contact lenses in for almost eighteen hours, and now my eyes were terribly sore. My corneas were obviously scratched. It felt as though someone was rubbing sandpaper across my eyeballs. Lynda called the doctor and got a prescription for an ointment. Even so, I had to keep my eyes shut the rest of the day.

September 10

I finally was able to open my eyes in midafternoon and found that I hadn't been dreaming for ten days. I had lost two games to the Russians. The newspaper columnists were giving it to us again with both barrels. John Robertson wrote that the overpriced hockey players were getting criticized for once and so they acted childishly. It's quite an eye-opener to see how this series is affecting different people. After all, did anyone reasonably believe we were going to be down 2–1–1 after four games? Now a lot of people have been psyched out by the Russians because they're so strong. So well trained. So well coached. So well prepared. So damn good. And they've got us charted. Will it ever end?

September 11

I spent the day at McGill Law School working out a schedule for the final semester. If all goes well, I will finish law school next year.

September 12

We're back together again. I flew to Toronto this morning and joined the rest of the players for a reception at the Labatts brewery, not a bad place for a reception. Labatts is the major sponsor of the series telecasts, having paid some eight hundred thousand dollars to get its commercials on the tube. They'll probably have to sell more than three million bottles of beer just to recoup that money.

I also had a meeting with Tim Turner, an engineer with General Electric of Canada, who brought down some face masks he has been developing for me. I'm not satisfied with my present mask because it's not very protective. I want a mask that extends farther back, providing more protection at the temple areas, and also one that will absorb the shot better. Tim had turned out a prototype that solved the problems of energy absorption and protection, but it was rather ugly looking. No goaltender will buy an ugly mask, because it will attract the attention, and the abuse, of his teammates and rivals. So we changed the exterior a bit, drilled a few holes without altering the protective features, and now we think we have a very protective, very marketable mask. I'm taking the new mask with me, and I'll start using it in practice.

September 13

The seats in the Frankfurt airport are comfortable, thank goodness. I can't sleep on cars, buses, trains, planes — anything that moves — so I spent most of the long flight from Toronto working on paper for a law class. I also had a chance to talk with Jim Taylor, a sports columnist in Vancouver, about the reaction of the fans in Vancouver last Friday night. Jim said he was ashamed of them. Still, I think Alan Eagleson went overboard a little when he said that the Vancouver fans showed a lack of class and suggested that Vancouver might be overlooked in the scheduling of future Canada-Russia games. Al is an impulsive guy, and I'm sure he made his comments in anger. I'm sure the people in Montreal, Toronto, Winnipeg, or anywhere else would have reacted the same way under the same circumstances.

We had a seven-hour layover in Frankfurt before boarding a connecting flight to Stockholm. (The other half of the team, meanwhile, was in Paris waiting for another flight to Stockholm.) I slept for about an hour in the airport, woke up, started to read James Dickey's *Deliverance,* and then decided to buy a camera at the duty-free shop. But I changed my mind when I discovered how brutally expensive cameras are even in Germany. Instead, I phoned a friend who is with the Canadian Army in Baden-Baden and asked him if he could get me one at his PX. Before leaving for Stockholm we had one minor incident: the Brothers Esposito could not find their passports. After an anxious search, one of the Air Canada agents found them underneath some seats on the plane we had taken over from Toronto. Heck, Tony and Phil could do a lot for the West German hockey team.

At the Stockholm airport the Swedish press cornered Phil Esposito and badgered him with a few thousand questions. Phil is a big name here, not only because of his accomplishments in the NHL but also because he endorses a European-market helmet that apparently is the most popular type of headgear in Sweden. I never realized that Phil wore a helmet!

We bused downtown to the Grand, an old-style class hotel right near the royal palace and the parliament buildings. The Grand is perched on an inlet of the Baltic and offers one of the most pleasing views I've ever seen. We met with Harry and Fergy to get our training schedules, and right after that I went to bed.

September 14

Double sessions again. It was very cool inside the rink at the Johanneshovs Isstadion, a pleasant change from the humidity back in Canada. I felt good, but I had no energy. No staying power. No conditioning. I hadn't been on the ice in almost six days, and I felt it.

The ice surface is some twelve feet wider than the rinks back home, but it's about the same length as our rinks. The four corners are pretty squared, so there's much more room behind the nets. We're told that the rink in Moscow is practically a duplicate of the Isstadion. So we will have to make some technical adjustments in our playing styles before leaving for Moscow next week.

In the NHL, for instance, most players position themselves according to the proximity of the sideboards, but if they do that here, they will be spreading themselves too wide and will find themselves out of shooting range. Instead, they will have to concentrate on playing sound, positional hockey in relationship to the net and forget about the location of the boards. Defensively, I think our guys are worrying that the extra width will let the smaller and speedier Soviet players skate wide around them for easy shots on the goal. After a couple of days' practice, though, I think they'll discover that their fears are unwarranted. You *want* to force the shooters wide on the bigger rink because it takes away their good shooting angle.

One thing that puzzled me about Tretiak's play in Canada was that he never went around behind the net to stop the puck and leave it for his defensemen. Now I know why. The distance from the goal line to the end boards here is at least five feet longer than in North American rinks. It seems like a two-day trip to get to the puck and then back to the crease. I can see that we will not have time enough to go around behind the net and stop the puck ourselves.

This particular problem could require the greatest adjustment in our technique. In the NHL there is little organized play behind the net, just a lot of bumping and muscling for loose pucks. Here, though, you can play a whole game behind the net. You *can* handle the puck. You *can* create plays. You can do everything but shoot. To me, at least, it seems like a more logical way to play the game. Give the puck to a winger in the corner during a power play, and he can hold it for twenty or thirty seconds while waiting for his teammates to get in position for a pass or a rebound.

I'm playing very stupidly. It seems that I've hit rock bottom. I'm doing everything wrong. My confidence is zilch. I've forgotten how to play the game. I'm guessing on shots. Sure, at certain times you do have to guess. When someone is in close and has a very clear shot, you must anticipate the spot where the shot probably will go if you expect to have any chance for making the save. Fine. But the danger lies in anticipating too much, and that's what I'm now doing.

It's pretty easy for a goaltender to fall into this predicament, especially in practice sessions, where he is somewhat familiar with the shots and the moves of the people who have the puck. It does not matter whether he is facing an average NHL player or a star; most players will make the same play under similar circumstances. Consequently, goaltenders can make educated guesses about what puck carriers probably will do in given situations. For this reason alone, goaltenders often seem to get better with age. They certainly don't get any faster, they just become a lot smarter and begin to move instinctively as situations develop because they have faced the same play by the same player countless times before. The danger, though, lies in guessing when you don't have to guess. When you start doing that, forwards recognize it, abandon their normal pattern, and embarrass you. The Espositos and the Ratelles don't usually fall into shooting patterns. Just when you think they always shoot the puck low to your left, they beat you with an easy shot high to the right. Do you ever feel dumb.

Today in practice, Red Berenson came at me from the left wing. Red has a very good backhand shot and likes to cut across and flip a backhander over the goalie's left hand — my glove hand — into the top corner. He does this so well that even when you know what he's going to do, it still is very difficult to stop. This time I didn't wait for Red to make his move but guessed what he would do. I flew across the goal mouth from right to left and then shot my glove up high.

Red recognized immediately what I was doing. So this time he pretended that he was going to try his favorite maneuver and then, at the last instant, he simply dribbled the puck along the ice and into the net between my right skate and the post. Meanwhile, I was at the other side of the cage with my left hand stuck up in midair. It was really embarrassing.

Ulf Sterner, probably the best Swedish player, watched our practice. I'm told that he had the talent to play in the NHL but that he was treated unmercifully by the other professionals when he played a few games for the New York Rangers during the mid-sixties. Europeans, particularly Swedes, have a reputation for being something less than courageous against the boards and in the corners. As a result, the pros tested Ulfie time after time with their high sticks, and finally it got to him, understandably, and he returned to Sweden. When I watched him play against the Canadian National Team three years ago he seemed very nervous. I suspect that Ulfie never has recovered from his NHL experience.

After our afternoon workout we stayed on the ice and gave a clinic for some Swedish kids. On the whole, our practice techniques are not too impressive, and I think the young boys sensed that. We do a few gimmicky things — like rapid-fire shots at the goaltenders from ten and fifteen feet away — that might impress sympathetic North Americans ("Geez, that poor goalie"), but European drills are much more advanced. The Swedish team, for instance, works on game-type situations during practice. Not us. Too often we practice such things as three-on-nothing breaks. Now how often do you see a three-on-nothing during a game?

The Swedish press has apparently changed its feeling about Canadian hockey players. When the National Team used to come to Stockholm, the papers always were filled with stories saying: "The Canadian animals are back in town." We received the worst press imaginable. The Swedes can give very definite reasons for hating the Canadians. They think that the Canadian style of hockey, with its physical contact and its questionable amount of high-sticking, is totally repugnant. They prefer a skating game, with a minimum of physical contact. What generally happened in our games was that the Canadian players stopped the Swedes with some violent physical tactics. The next day the papers would be filled with cartoons depicting the Canadians as animals.

But we are the pros, not the amateurs and not the animals, and the Swedes have invited us. Also, the two games this weekend are the highlights of the fiftieth anniversary celebration of ice hockey in Sweden. So the

Phil Esposito, our leader, pleads a hopeless cause with one
of the officials.

Swedes now are catering to us, doing all they can to make us feel at home.

After practice there was still another reception, this time at the residence of Margaret Meagher, the Canadian ambassador to Sweden. She lives in a very large house on a small lake outside the city. The embassy itself is in a beautiful building downtown. It seems pretty incongruous to me, because I can't imagine that Canada needs such lavish facilities here in Sweden. We don't trade that much with Sweden because we mainly market the same things: pulp, paper, and wood. Also, I don't imagine that Stockholm is a sensitive diplomatic post.

The reception also became a birthday party for Harry Sinden. Harry turned forty today, though I'll bet he has aged about twenty years in the last month. All in all, it was a good affair, unlike the normal diplomatic cocktail party, because the embassy staffers here in Stockholm are level, down-to-earth types who don't act like diplomats.

At the reception a Swedish coach, Lasse Lillje, asked me if I would be interested in teaching at a hockey school here next summer. I think I would. There's a big difference between European hockey schools and North American hockey schools, which are really summer camps with hockey as the main activity. At home, the teaching is minimal, with just two or three hours of ice time each day and mediocre instruction at best. Scrimmaging, not teaching. Personally, I think we may be underestimating the North American youngster. Maybe he really wants to learn.

The European schools are much more advanced. They work on techniques in drills, then apply them in scrimmages. Players spend seven or eight hours a day with hockey, but they don't just play hockey. There are periods of physical conditioning, blackboard talks, and closed-circuit television instruction. Lasse told me that he felt the only area where Europeans can learn from North American techniques is goaltending. The Russians said the same thing and then introduced Mr. Tretiak.

September 15

We had two more brutal practices. I'm still on the skids and can't brake myself. I'm getting lower and lower. This is really the worst point of the series for me. Montreal and Vancouver may have been discouraging, but I still had the feeling of "okay, I've got work to do." Now I've lost that feeling. The Moscow games look like a frightening prospect right now. We all seem bored with the whole thing. We're tired and want to relax, but we can't.

It's fairly obvious, too, that having thirty-five players here in Stockholm is a mistake. In some ways you really need thirty-five players: for scrimmages, for instance, and for providing at least some competition for places in the lineup. In other ways it's a disaster. A lot of players can sense they will not be playing in Moscow. It is natural to expect these guys to go out and have a good time. This has a contagious effect on the guys who *are* playing or who *might be* playing. Later, those who don't expect to play *do* play — and aren't ready.

There is also a psychological problem. From the very beginning, the Sweden trip had been held out as an eight-day vacation from the grind of the series. That was when we felt that the Russian games would not be that difficult, that we would roll through them without much trouble in Canada. Now the Canada games have gone badly, so instead of a vacation in Sweden this should be a time to make strides for the games in Mos-

[99]

cow. Unfortunately, as of now, it is not proving to be that way. Personally, I don't think it's very sensible for a team to go on the road for eight days. You don't relax on the road. You do go out at night. And the combination of boredom and these other things makes for lackadaisical practices and sagging spirits. I suspect that Harry and Fergy have pretty much the same thoughts right now.

I played for twenty minutes in an intrasquad scrimmage and didn't give up any goals. For the first time in weeks I felt in command. I tried to force the shooters to beat me by staying more in my net, and it worked for twenty minutes. One thing that helped was the circle that forms the goaltender's crease on European hockey rinks. In North America, of course, the crease is a rectangle, and goalies use the leading corners to maintain their bearings. In Sweden and Russia the crease is a half-moon — with no corners. So I had to remain in my net or risk losing my bearings. Whether or not that change was the reason, I didn't fish any pucks out of the net, and that was quite an improvement.

Later, I walked around Stockholm for a couple of hours. It's a pleasant city, surrounded by inlets, but it does not have any great museums or many places of great historical significance, at least for North Americans. I stopped in a park and watched some men playing chess on the biggest board I have ever seen. The pawns must have been a foot high and the knights and bishops were at least two feet tall. One man even had to get up from his chair, pick up a knight, and walk around the table to set it down in another position.

One thing I don't like about Sweden is the prices. Three kronor — about sixty-five cents — for a Coke, ten kronor for a bottle of beer. Later on, my father arrived from Oslo, Norway, and we had dinner together. I told him not to expect any miracles in Moscow.

September 16

Game tonight against the Swedish National Team, but not for me. I practiced with the Black Aces this morning and spent most of the time ducking hard shots around my head. When a guy knows he's not playing that night, he takes his aggressions out on the puck and the goaltender. Afterwards, I chatted with some Swedish hockey officials about the life styles of their players.

Sterner and goaltender Leif Holmquist, who is recovering from knee surgery, are Sweden's highest-paid "amateurs," getting more than twenty thousand dollars a year for just playing hockey. The average player, though, earns only some six thousand dollars and must maintain a full-time job to support himself and his family. After all, six thousand dollars does not go very far in Sweden, not when Coke costs sixty-five cents a can. Sterner, though, is leaving in a few days to play with the Chicago Cougars of the World Hockey Association. Another good Swedish player, defenseman Thommis Bergman, quit the Nationals two weeks ago and now is trying to win a job with the Detroit Red Wings.

Since the game was not scheduled to start until 9:30 P.M., the Black Aces practiced again at 6 P.M. Before we left for the rink, Harry told us not to wear our Team Canada blazers around Stockholm. He is afraid, I guess, that Swedish photographers will tail us around town and snap our pictures the minute we do anything out of the ordinary.

As I watched the game from the stands, it was immediately obvious that the Swedes had not changed one iota since the last time I played against them. They are terribly frustrating to play; indeed, it's impossible not to become emotional. Swedes are justifiably known for their melodrama on the ice, particularly for the way they take dives. It's one thing to do a neat little swan dive in hopes of getting a penalty. It's another thing to do a triple gainer or a quadruple somersault off the fifty-meter board. That's what the Swedes do.

When you trip them even accidentally, they flop onto the ice and lay stretched out for what seems like hours. Our team is not used to such histrionics. In the NHL, anyone who puts on the big act violates the unwritten code. Actors are ostracized in NHL dressing rooms.

We won 4–1. For some reason I was nervous throughout the game. Against the Russians I never have time to get nervous because everything happens so quickly. Here, though, I could spot mistakes a few seconds before they happened — so I worried about them. The Swedes played worse than I had ever seen them. I think they abandoned their style. Maybe they lacked confidence, or were afraid of the aggressive professionals.

The game clearly pointed out the different attitudes of the Canadians and the Swedes towards the referees. In Canada, the referees invariably get booed when their names are announced at the start of a game. In Sweden, though, the referees are cheered like returning heroes. The Swedes never protest more than mildly a referee's decision during the game, while Canadian players, on the other hand, like to berate the officials in jaw-to-jaw discussions. It's basically a part of the North American attitude; the player knows he cannot change the referee's decision but he hopes to influence the next one. In this regard, it is easy to understand why Swedes picture us as bad-mannered crybabies.

The highlight of the game, as far as the Black Aces were concerned, was the commercials flashed on the ice surface between periods. The lights went out and a giant projector flashed huge commercial messages on the ice. The best one showed a rather attractive girl nude from the waist up as a come-on for a tabloid.

September 17

Harry skated over to me at the Black Aces practice this morning and said, "You're playing." Then I was almost knocked out. There was a skirmish around the net and I fell against the crossbar. If it weren't for my new mask I would have taken the count, but all I got was a scratch on the mask.

As it turned out, what Harry had meant by "you're playing" was that I would be the backup goalie for Eddie Johnston. This did not turn out to be fun. First of all, I could hardly see from the bench because the boards were too high and the bench was too low. I tried standing, but that was very tiring. Then I brought a chair from the dressing room and propped it on the bench, which didn't work either. Finally I ended up kneeling on the bench, for a long, uncomfortable couple of hours.

While we did not play well last night, we played even worse tonight. Harry and Fergy used almost all the Black Aces, and many of the guys had not worked in a game since last March or April. We played poorly and took a lot of stupid penalties. Naturally we did a lot of crying about these penalties, too. Actually, I think we deserved at least eighty percent of them; certainly they would have been called by NHL referees. But we cried about them and lost our composure. If Eddie Johnston had not been sensational in the goal the Swedes would have chased us out of Scandinavia. As it was, Phil Esposito had to score a shorthanded goal in the last minute of play to get us a 4–4 tie.

It's about time we stop bitching about European referees. NHL and international rules are practically identical; they differ only in the way the officials interpret them. It is only natural that referees working for different organizations will interpret the rules differently. For instance, in college hockey in the United States, the western referees permit a much more physical game than the eastern officials. You must adjust to it, that's all.

The biggest difference now is interference, which is always a two-minute penalty in the NHL but is somewhat permissible in international play. European refereeing may not be great, but it is as consistent as North American officiating. It is no fluke that a particular call is made at a particular time. If it's a penalty, then it's a penalty. We knew that European referees would be handling the games in Stockholm and Moscow, and we accepted that fact. Now we should accept the consequences and adjust accordingly. Canadian teams have been complaining about European referees ever since international play began; it would seem reasonable that we would begin to get the idea that European refereeing is not going to change to adjust to our style.

Here, though, is a classic example why the two-referee system — two officials with equal authority — used in international amateur competition is hardly sensible. Jean Ratelle upset a Swedish player in the corner. Okay, maybe Ratelle tripped him. The referee closest to the play, about ten feet away, waved "no penalty" by spreading his hands in the traditional safe sign. The other referee, who was way over on the other side of the ice, at least fifty feet away from the play, then waved his left hand at Ratelle and raised his right hand in the air, signifying that Ratelle would get a penalty as soon as Team Canada controlled the puck. Needless to say, we argued pretty vehemently with the officials. Why did one referee wave "no penalty" and the other signal for the penalty? If the first referee had been smart he would not have given the safe signal in the first place.

During the game there were also numerous examples of the different hockey philosophies of the Swedish and the Canadian players. Two examples:

1) The ethic of the North American pro is to hide pain, not display it. Being cut or injured is accepted as part of the game, not a reason to become a thespian. When a baseball pitcher hits the batter with a pitch, the batter rarely rubs the spot where the ball hit him, because he doesn't want to give the pitcher the satisfaction of thinking that he's hurt. In hockey, Serge Savard skated off the ice on a broken leg once, and Bobby Baun of the Toronto Maple Leafs played two periods of a Stanley Cup game with a broken ankle.

Tonight, Cashman and Sterner crashed into the boards together near the end of the first period. In self-defense Sterner lifted his stick and caught Cash in the mouth with it. Cash started to bleed profusely, because the blade of the stick had slit his tongue down the middle, but most people didn't even know he was injured. Cash calmly skated to the bench, remained there for the rest of the period, and then skated unobtrusively to the dressing room. The doctors treated the injury, and after that Cash changed into his civilian clothes and watched the rest of the game from alongside our bench.

In the last period, with about six minutes left in the game, Vic Hadfield caught Lars-Erik Sjoberg with a high stick and cut him around the nose. Sjoberg gave it the real Hollywood performance for about five minutes. He waved off the trainer, then started to skate slowly towards his bench as the blood streamed unchecked from his nose. The fans were screaming at Hadfield, who was in the penalty box by now, and then Sjoberg changed his course and skated past the penalty box himself. With one hand he waved at Hadfield, and with the other he pointed to his bleeding nose. Finally he went to his bench and leaned against the boards for a few minutes before taking a seat on the bench. After the next whistle, Sjoberg left the bench and skated ever so slowly towards his dressing room, all the time holding a towel not on the bloody nose but in his hand. The crowd cheered Sjoberg as he left the ice. Was he finished with his act? No. Playing the hero's role perfectly, he waited at the bottom of the ramp so the Swedish photographers could take pictures of the nose from a zillion different angles.

2) All game long the Swedes were what NHL players snidely call "snow throwers." When a Swede thought he was about to be hit by one of our players, he braked to a snow-throwing halt in order to avoid the collision. The Swedes prefer to avoid contact at any cost. On the other hand, the most damnable thing an NHL player can be called is a "snow thrower." Yet, this is perfectly consistent with the Swedes' entire approach. If they view us as being overly aggressive, then it only makes sense to avoid a physical confrontation.

September 18

Predictably, Lars-Erik Sjoberg's battered nose was all over the front pages of all the Stockholm papers. One paper showed separate pictures of the broken nose (which wasn't really broken) and the black eye. There were no pictures of Cashman in the papers, but Cash is in the hospital now. His tongue swelled up last night;

he had a tough time breathing; and he had to be fed intravenously.

The honeymoon with the Swedish press is definitely over. We are animals again. Sterner even wrote a story in which he called us "gangsters." And the Canadian ambassador, Margaret Meagher, is on us, too. She too suggested that we behaved like animals. Alan Eagleson did not take too kindly to her remarks and in a not-too-polite tone told her to mind her own business.

Ted Blackman of the *Montreal Gazette* had a funny comment about the whole thing. "Gee," he said to me, "that handshake after the game last night really meant something. Like, ah, sorry, friend, that I tried to poke your eye out. Sorry I hit you over the head with my stick."

Later on, I ran into Eagleson at a restaurant. I was really down, lower than ever, for myself but more for the team. We had played terribly against the Swedes, and I knew if we played that way in Russia we'd get bombed. As I talked with Eagleson, a Swedish man interrupted our conversation to ask — not in an outraged voice, but sort of sadly — why we had played so roughly against his team. I don't think anyone can answer that question, but Eagleson tried: "Certain things acceptable here in Sweden are not acceptable in Canada," he said. "You people are good with your sticks, particularly with spearing. Spearing is the worst of sins in Canada; it's not even part of the hatchet man's style. And fighting is part of our game but not part of yours. We just play two completely different games." I don't think the man understood completely, but he dropped the subject and said: "You'll lose in Russia." Al replied: "No. We won't lose, because despite all the things we have going against us, we still have it here." He pointed to his heart.

Talking about getting bombed, someone phoned our

hotel Saturday night after the game and said a bomb would explode at midnight. False alarm.

September 19

I understand that the Canadian papers are getting on us for our lack of conditioning and the fact that we seem to be spending a lot of time out on the town. They are bailing out again. Pierre Gobeil of *Montreal Matin* wrote one day: "I am ashamed to be a Canadian." What has happened in Sweden has been disappointing and does provide reason for self-analysis. But from the players' standpoint it doesn't help to be an alarmist. It's one thing for writers to report what they see and perceive regarding conditioning and mental preparedness, but all the sentimental overbearing serves no purpose.

One thing that has become very obvious is that Bobby Orr will not be playing in Moscow. His knee still flares up after he skates, so the doctors don't even want him to scrimmage. Today he was walking in downtown Stockholm and almost fell over when the knee suddenly locked. You can see that being a spectator does not agree with Bobby. He takes his treatments, then comes down for all the practices, standing around the boards and yelling encouragement to the players. During the workout today Bobby kept talking to Yvan Cournoyer about our power play, or our lack of power play. Bobby thinks we're rushing things, that we're trying to score too quickly when we get a man advantage. "Take your time, take your time," he kept telling Yvan during the workout. "No hurry. No hurry. They won't be coming after you."

September 20

I've resigned myself to the fact that I probably won't
be playing in Moscow. Tony played very well the first
game in Stockholm, and Eddie was superb in the second
game. They'll probably split the games in Russia. Now
I'll have to think about getting myself ready for the
start of the NHL season. We still have a whole season to
play.

And so we're off to Moscow at last. If we ever play this
series again, I'm certain Team Canada won't spend eight
days in Stockholm.

Our plane was late, naturally, and while we waited
at the Stockholm airport Ted Blackman made the rounds
and talked to all the players. "What's your rush," I said
to him. "We've still got ten more days together." He
shook his head. "No, we don't. Your wives will have all
the newspaper clippings waiting for you in Moscow, and
when you guys read them you won't talk to us again.
I've got to do some serious fence-mending right now before it's too late."

It was almost 8 P.M. when we finally landed in Moscow. The Canadian ambassador, Robert Ford, met us at
the ramp, and then we boarded a bus for the fifty-yard
trip to the terminal. Knowing Russian efficiency, I figured
we'd spend an hour or two sitting on the bus waiting for
the clerks to check our passports, unload our luggage, and
clear us through immigration. However, as it turned out,
they needed only fifteen minutes to clear us — record
time.

We must be celebrities or something. One of the Air
Canada men at the airport told us that Boris Spassky was
delayed several hours by airport and customs officials

when he returned to Moscow after losing his chess championship to Bobby Fischer.

I sat alongside a window during the bus ride into Moscow and kept looking out for one of the massive steel tank traps that the Russians had erected along some main roads to the city. There it was: crossed beams wrapped with barbed wire. So striking. The tank traps identify the spots where the Russians finally repulsed Hitler's invasion during the early days of World War II. The closest point is within about twenty-five minutes of downtown Moscow.

We also passed by the Central Army Club, the big Dynamo soccer stadium and the Science Institute, where the Soviet cosmonauts prepare for their trips into outer space. Finally, the bus rolled onto Gorki Street and pulled up in front of the Hotel Intourist, a twenty-two-story maze of glass and steel that is the latest thing in Moscow hotels. My wife, Lynda, was waiting there with all the other wives, and suddenly the hotel lobby seemed like Place Ville Marie at midday as hundreds and hundreds of Canadians welcomed the players with raised champagne goblets.

Before checking in, however, the players went off and had dinner in a private room on the second floor. The steak, surprisingly, was excellent, much better than the tasteless veal I had to eat three times a day in Leningrad a couple of years ago. After dinner I met Lynda again and we went for a walk through Red Square, which is about five hundred yards from the hotel. It was pretty chilly and I had left my raincoat on the plane in Frankfurt, so I practically froze as we watched the changing of the guard at Lenin's tomb and gawked at the massiveness of the Kremlin wall and the buildings behind it.

When we returned to the hotel, the lobby was still

crowded with Canadian fans, who now were trying to figure out what to do with themselves. In Moscow, tourists must buy liquor in the so-called dollar bars that accept only foreign currency in payment for the refreshments, and this night, anyway, the bars had run out of vodka and scotch and champagne. Rather than fight the crowds, we left the hotel and walked to the metro, but unfortunately we did not have any rubles or kopecks with us and could not get inside.

Our room at the Intourist is very adequate, a big improvement over the Metropole, which I stayed in the last time I was here.

September 21

The bus ride to the hockey rink brings you through much of the city. You pass by the Kremlin wall as you drive through one of the city's oldest sections, with blocks and blocks of peeling, pale yellow buildings. There are long lines outside an exhibition hall featuring a display of French paintings, but there are longer lines outside some markets and stores, as housewives queue up to buy special food products. You drive past the ultra-modern buildings that form the headquarters for the economic agencies of the socialist world. Then, as you turn off the main street and onto the road alongside the Moscow River that leads to the rink, the Ukraine Hotel stares at you like Big Brother. The Stalin regime went heavily neo-classic Gothic in building the Ukraine and five other massive buildings early in the 1950s. For years these buildings have been the butt of tourist jokes because of their antiquated style.

Five minutes later, after a pleasant riverside drive past an enormous chemical plant and a sixteenth-century structure — the New Maiden Cemetery and Monastery — that is in the process of being restored, you finally reach the Lenin Sports Complex in Luzhnicki. This vast area at the foot of the Lenin Hills contains a one-hundred-thousand-seat soccer stadium, the fourteen-thousand-seat Palace of Sport hockey rink, two swimming pools, several dozen tennis and basketball courts and two bandy rinks.

The hockey stadium itself is unique. The seating area is rectangular, so that the sections at the ends of the rink are not rounded at all. The rink itself is not centered in this rectangle, so about forty percent of all the seats are at one end of the rink, behind the goal line. The first row of seats is about fifteen feet from the boards on the sides and about one hundred feet from the boards at one end. The people in the far corner might as well be sitting in Kiev or Stockholm. The three thousand Canadians who are here for the series all have seats in the far end, but what else did they expect? The seats, by the way, are not seats but contoured benches.

The Russian team was practicing on the ice, so I sat in the stands to watch them and survey the playing surface. Instead of unbreakable glass, the Russians have put netting on top of the boards behind the goals. This will cause some problems because pucks will boomerang off the taut netting with a slingshot effect. I watched one puck rebound off the netting all the way out past the blue line on the fly. The ice surface itself is some seven feet wider but the same length as most NHL rinks. Contrary to my expectations, the corners are not squared and I doubt that we'll be able to set up plays from them as we had planned in Stockholm.

Surprisingly, the distance between the goal line and the backboards is as short as in NHL rinks. About half the distance of the Stockholm rink. So why doesn't Tretiak go around behind his net and stop the puck for his defensemen? I thought I had figured out the answer in Stockholm. Now I don't know.

I had to laugh, though, when I saw all the signs that had been painted on the boards. Most Russians probably have never seen a commercial or an advertisement of any sort. Yet there are sixteen messages on the boards now, selling everything from Jockey shorts to turtle wax to Heineken beer. Every time, say, Brad Park and Boris Mikhailov fight for a puck near the blue line, the Canadian television cameras will pan in on the action and the viewers back home will be able to see the battle between Park and Mikhailov as well as an advertisement for Ski-Doo snowmobiles. The Russians have charged twelve thousand dollars for each message — that's a total of two hundred thousand dollars for the sixteen — and I understand they had to cancel a lucrative deal they had made for the choice spot at center ice. What happened was that Molson's Brewery bought the space at center ice for twenty-five thousand dollars. Labatts, which, of course, is paying about eight hundred thousand dollars to sponsor the telecasts back in Canada, found out about it and called Eagleson. Al, in turn, phoned the Russians, and now the Molson's sign has disappeared. How would it look for the announcers to be selling Labatts while the cameras were focused on Molson's?

After a while I went to our dressing rooms — one was not big enough for thirty-five players, so we had a whole suite of rooms — and got dressed for practice. I came back while they were still cleaning and resurfacing the ice and was amazed to see that they use two machines for the job. "Two do the job twice as fast," someone said seriously. The ice itself is very deep, perhaps as thick as three inches. The normal depth of the ice on a North American rink is probably half an inch, with an absolute maximum of five-eighths of an inch. As a result of the thickness, the ice was too hard and very chippy.

Up in the stands, the Russian players watched our very listless practice, all dressed in the blue sweat suits with the thin white stripe down the side that Soviet athletes seem to wear everyplace they go, including movie theaters and restaurants. Maybe they will become overconfident.

Tretiak sat away from his teammates on the other side of the rink with Anatoli Tarasov, the man who has done more for Russian hockey than anyone else. Tarasov coached the Russian National Team to more than a dozen world championships and four Olympic gold medals, but last March he was suddenly replaced by Bobrov. According to rumors, Tarasov asked for a pay raise and got the axe instead. Now he coaches the Soviet Army Club in Russia's major hockey league. Tretiak is his No. 1 goaltender, and eleven of his regulars play for the Soviet National Team. As you might guess, the Soviet Army Club always finishes in first place, or it has for nine of the last ten years.

Eagleson was chatting with Tretiak and Tarasov, and he introduced the goaltender to Jean Beliveau. "You know of Mr. Beliveau, don't you?" Eagleson said to Tretiak. "Yes, yes," Tretiak said through an interpreter. Beliveau laughed and said, "And I know of you, too." Eagleson and Tretiak were kidding about an invitation to Bobby Orr's hockey camp in Ontario next summer. "You would pay to bring my wife, too?" Tretiak asked Eagleson. Alan replied, "You're becoming quite the professional already. Next you'll want to know about the pension plan."

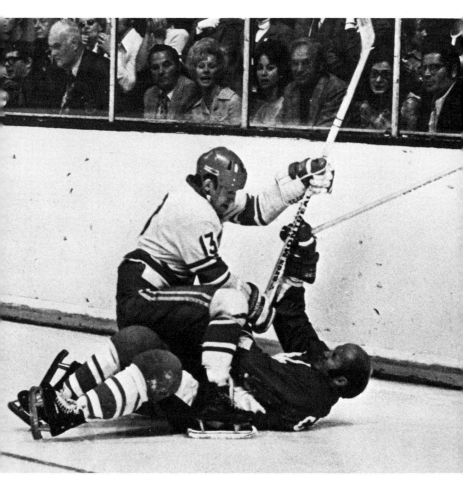

Boris Mikhailov (13) and Gary Bergman had a little
disagreement in Toronto.

On our way back to the hotel everyone was talking about a trade. Toronto had sent Jim McKenney, a defenseman, to Minnesota for goaltender Gump Worsley. "I haven't talked to Jim Gregory [the Toronto general manager] yet today," said Harold Ballard, the owner of the Leafs, "but we need a goalie and Gump's damn good." Bruce Norris, the owner of the Detroit Red Wings, congratulated Ballard on making a good deal.

Steak again for lunch, which is not a bad way to go. Unfortunately, our wives are not having the same luck with their meals. We brought along our own steaks, but they have to eat the hotel's daily fare. A lot of the players are going back for seconds and taking doggy bags filled with steak and bread out to their wives, but I always forget or end up eating the seconds myself. Lynda's not very happy about it.

We played tourist again for a few hours, visiting St. Basil's Cathedral and GUM, which is opposite Lenin's tomb in Red Square. It is the largest single shopping place in the world, covering more than three city blocks. After dinner — another steak — we all went to see the Moscow Circus. I had seen the circus in 1969, and at that time it was housed in a decrepit building that looked more like a cinema hall. Now the circus has a new home, very beautiful and very elaborate, out on Moscow Hills, just across the road from Moscow University. The highlight of the performance was an incredible aerial act climaxed by a death-defying leap from nowhere into a long, thin, hardly visible net.

Back at the hotel, Vic Hadfield, Rick Martin and Jocelyn Guevremont came around to say good-bye. Rumors had been circulating that we might be having some defections, but I couldn't believe they were true. Thinking about it, I don't understand how a player can leave. Sure, I'm certain some people are hurt and disappointed that they have not been playing, but at the same time what can they gain by going home? We are all part of a team and presumably should have some interest in how things are going around here. The alternative to staying here and cheering on the team is going home to training camp and facing a lot of criticism. They will be returning to something they have gone through before, playing meaningless games in small cities before small audiences. To me it seems incomprehensible. But it's their decision, and I'm sure in their own minds they think they're right.

September 22

Forget that McKenney for Worsley deal. It was a rumor. One trouble with being in Moscow is that there are no English-language dailies to let you know what's happening on the other side of the world. Someone started the McKenney-Worsley talk, and most people bought it since it was a semibelievable deal. Today's rumor, compliments of Fergy and E. J., by the way, is Carl Eller for Ted Kwalick. You can't believe anyone anymore. We practiced again in the morning, and I seemed to play fairly well, but I don't expect to play again until the opening game of the NHL season next month.

I had a Coke fit in the dressing room after the workout. You don't know how satisfying a Coke tastes after a long workout, but, *sacrebleu*, there were no Cokes available. "Tomorrow," the trainers told me. If I had been smart I would have done what all the other guys did: they bought extra luggage packs at the Stockholm airport and filled them with six-packs of Coke and something called Jolly Cola from Denmark. One of the guys told me there was a roomful of Coke in Room 1774 of the Intourist. But that was just another idle rumor. There will be Cokes for the players after the game tonight, though. Come to think of it, that's a heck of an incentive to get into the starting lineup.

Outside the Palace of Sports, hundreds of young Russian boys cluster around us as we walk to and from our bus. The Russian kids like to play the Button Game. They come up to you with, say, a lapel button showing the hammer and sickle and indicate by hand signals they'd like to make a deal. At the start we had to establish the going rates for various Soviet buttons. A stick of Wrigley's Spearmint for the hammer and sickle was perfectly acceptable to the Russians. A maple-leaf button for a *Pravda* pin was equitable, too. A broken hockey stick, though, would bring up to ten badges or two Lenin buttons, supposedly the toughest buttons for the Russian kids to get themselves. Bobby Orr became pretty unpopular with the guys when he traded a good hockey stick for just one Lenin button. "Stop underselling us, Orr," Phil Esposito complained. "You're spoiling things." Bobby also traded maple-leaf buttons like crazy; in fact, he had about a hundred of them pinned to his T-shirt for sudden deals.

Later on, I picked up the *Moscow News,* an English-language weekly, and read an interview some writer had with Vsevolod Bobrov. The translation was very stilted, and I wondered whether the writer interviewed Bobrov or the minister of Sports Propaganda. Believe it or not, there is such a man with that title. After saying that his team had much to learn from the Canadians about conducting a power play (is he serious?), Bobrov went on to comment: "In Moscow we are placing our main stake on our young players, for one can hardly think of a better way to study than by playing against Canada." And in finishing the interview Bobrov added, "The Canadians have studied their errors in the first games and are thoroughly prepared to take revenge. They have to salvage their tottering prestige as invincible players."

First of all, I think Soviets have a way of treating all sport as a continuous learning experience. They always seem to be analyzing and assessing tactics and techniques, their own and the opposition's. I'm convinced that their main goal in this series is to learn, even though many others believe they duped us. However, in Canada, their best players were the younger ones. Their worst defensemen were Aleksander Ragulin and Viktor Kuzkin, the oldest players on the team. So the "main stake" that Bobrov talks about is really the sensible stake.

Regarding his other point — that we have studied our errors — right now I'm not convinced that we have studied and corrected them. I don't think we're thoroughly prepared to take revenge, as Bobrov claims. As a matter of fact, I'm not very confident about our chances for success in the next four games.

I went to the rink early so I could watch the Russians warm up. In North America, the pregame exercise consists of a brief skate around one-half the ice, seven or eight minutes of target practice against the goaltenders, and some waves to friends in the seats. The Russians, though, have a highly disciplined, highly organized series of drills that would tire out a lot of professional teams.

Take Tretiak. After a brief skate, he moves into his net and does some stretching exercises. Then he begins his warm-up. It starts with Vladimir Shadrin lining up seven or eight pucks about twelve feet away and then rapidly firing them at preplanned spots. He'll fire ten straight shots low to Tretiak's left, then ten more high to his right. Tretiak knows where Shadrin will be shooting, which seems to defeat the purpose of a warm-up, but at the same time he gets himself into the habit of moving in the right way to stop the type of shot he will see most often in the game. He rehearses his moves; simultaneously, he familiarizes himself with the net. Very sensible, if you ask me. And something I have never thought about. After Shadrin finishes, Tretiak skates off to a corner and practices splitting onto the ice and then getting back up instantly.

Meanwhile, the Russian forwards and defensemen work on game-type situations like three-on-twos and two-on-ones, and get into the habit of passing the puck around and stickhandling out of the zone. They must use fifteen pucks during their warm-up; we use one or two. In one drill each player takes a puck and skates at full speed inside the zone, stickhandling all the time. It looks like a demolition derby as the players frantically try to avoid one another. At the same time it reminds them to keep their heads up and teaches puck control. At the end of the workout Tretiak looked exhausted. No wonder. He must have stopped two hundred shots. In fact, he'll probably be happy when the game begins because he won't have to work so hard.

It was going to be a noisy night. The three thousand Canadians arrived armed with air horns and whistles and leather lungs, and there were banners all over the place. One said "Mission Possible," for instance. There was a "Sarnia's Here, Whitey" banner for Pat Stapleton, too. And most of the Canadians were waving miniature Canadian flags. It was pretty exciting.

Across the ice, far away from the Canadian fans, the big three of Soviet politics — Leonid Brezhnev, Alexei Kosygin and Nikolai Podgorny — sat in the presidential box, while Yevgeny Yevtushenko, the great poet, was practically in the rafters. As the players skated side by side onto the ice, the fourteen thousand people in the

Palace of Sport stood and cheered wildly. The teams lined up at opposite blue lines, and then three dozen Soviet youngsters came onto the ice carrying beautiful floral bouquets for the players. The first player introduced was Phil Esposito, and he completely broke up the stiff pregame tension by stepping on a flower, tripping, and falling flat on the seat of his pants.

Phil was awfully embarrassed, I'm sure, but he handled the situation perfectly; as he got up he bowed good-naturedly to the crowd and smiled. Both teams almost fell over themselves with laughter.

The Russian fans behave much differently than their North American counterparts. For most of a game they sit on their hands, and as you look at them, all they seem to be is a sea of brown, black, and gray anonymity. They rarely clap or boo; if they think the referee has made a mistake or if they think the opposition is too rough, they whistle sharply. About the only encouragement they ever shout to their own players is the command *shaibu, shaibu. Shaibu* means puck, oddly enough; I guess they want their comrades to put the puck in the net.

Right off, I noticed a startling change in the Russians' style. In Canada their defensemen were primarily feeders; that is, they almost immediately passed the puck to their forwards. But in this game Yuri Liapkin and Vladimir Lutchenko, the best young Russian defensemen, rushed the puck themselves and shot it at the net from the blue line. At times Tretiak came out of his net and skated around to stop the puck for his defensemen. It seems he does this only when he feels like it, and when there won't be anything resembling a battle for the puck.

It is easy to detect the basketball influence, too, as their forwards set up picks around the net to keep our defensemen away from Tony Esposito. They have a player set up house near one of our defensemen, pass the puck off, and then stay in that position and block out our defenseman. Harry has told our forwards to do the same thing, but it's hard to break old habits so quickly.

We started out very strongly, forechecking the Russians closely and disrupting their slick passing game before they ever had a chance to get started. Late in the first period, Gilbert Perreault took a pass from Rod Gilbert and made a great move around Ragulin. Suddenly he whipped a perfect pass out to J. P. Parise in the slot and J. P. blasted the puck past Tretiak. J. P. was kidding about his goal-scoring touch before the game. "If you want to see a guy panic," he said, "just give me the puck in front of the net." He didn't panic this time.

Early in the second period Bobby Clarke cut in front of Tretiak from a different angle and stuffed the puck through his legs. 2–0. Then Henderson slapped in a rebound at 11:58 to make it 3–0. After the period Bill Good interviewed me on Canadian television and asked if I thought we'd have any difficulty protecting the lead during the final twenty minutes. "No," I said. "We've got the old adrenalin flowing now, and you don't get weary when there are three thousand fans cheering like crazy and you have a chance not only to win the game but also tie the series."

Then Good stunned me — and I'm sure his audience — when he asked if there were any chance that I'd be going home with Hadfield, Martin and Guevremont. What a stupid question! If the question had not taken me totally by surprise, I might have given him a verbal shot in return. Fortunately I answered his question in a polite way. But was I mad.

I don't think I'll ever forget what happened in the final twenty minutes. We played stupidly. Instead of continuing the forechecking tactics that had worked so well the first two periods, we stayed back and let the

Russians take the puck to us. Yuri Blinov promptly scored to cut the lead to 3–1, but Henderson scored again at the five-minute mark to restore our three-goal lead. That was all we could do. The Russians charged furiously. Anisin gave the Soviets some instant relief when he deflected a shot past Tony at 9:05, and then just eight seconds later Shadrin scooped up a loose puck and scored to cut our lead to 4–3. We were against the ropes now, waiting for the Soviet knockout punch.

Yvan Cournoyer twice had glittering chances on semi-breakaways — but he missed. Poor Yvan's in a little slump. I think he is trying to finesse the goaltenders instead of firing his hard, high shot at them. It's ironic, but I think part of Yvan's problem stems from listening to his own goalies. For years Yvan used to devastate them in practice sessions with his hard shots, and we finally convinced him to take it a bit easy on us. Now he's gotten into the habit of winding up, and then holding back and trying to make a play instead of a shot.

The Soviets finally tied the score at 11:41 as one of our defensemen accidentally tipped Aleksander Gusev's shot from the blue line over Tony's left shoulder. Then, three minutes later, they won the game on a pretty shot by Vladimir Vikulov after he stole the puck in the corner and skated across in front of Tony.

Our dressing room was absolutely silent. Total depression had set in. How could this thing happen? Phil Esposito looked over at me and said it was like the Boston-Montreal play-off game in 1971, when the Canadiens scored five third-period goals to win 7–5. We were all down. Here we were so enthusiastic half an hour before, and now were down 3–1–1 in the series and facing the bleak prospect of having to win the next three games to win the series.

Still, I can't say the Russians were lucky to win. They

are a very strong offensive team, not twenty guys dependent upon a star to bail them out. They never quit. They stuck to their normal, organized plan of attack, and eventually it paid off. Tretiak played very confidently. He obviously is very sure about his position in the net and about his ability to react to any given situation. I can't remember seeing him go down to make a save. For instance, one time Cournoyer came in on him and he simply braced himself in his position while Yvan danced back and forth trying to fake him out of the play. When the shot finally came, Tretiak handled it easily.

September 23

The Soviet press is giving it to us with both barrels. I guess that Harry was too upset to attend the postgame press conference last night (can you blame him?), so Tass wrote:

> It is hard to explain why the leader of the Canadian team of professionals was not present at the conference. One Canadian journalist suggested that Sinden decided he had no right leaving his players alone. Being on their own, the professional sportsmen can get depressed and then the outcome of the remaining matches will be decided. So Sinden immediately resorted to psychotherapy, regarding the task of preserving the morale of the team more important than politeness to newsmen.

I have picked up a bad cold, along with a case of the depressions. No more midnight walks in Red Square with only a sports coat for protection against the thirty-degree chill. As expected, practice was not the most cheerful couple of hours I have ever spent. No one really wanted to talk about what had happened the night before. Harry was still stunned. "We have our ups and downs," he said. "We play a good period, then a fair period, then a bad one. We can't put two good periods together, but the Russians could play the same way twenty-four hours a day until midnight of the third Tuesday next February." Midway through the workout I took a break and went over to the boards for a squirt of water.

"How are you feeling, big guy?" Fergy asked.

"Oh, all right, I guess," I answered, "but I'm still making stupid mistakes."

"Don't worry about them," Fergy said, "so long as you don't make them tomorrow night."

"What?"

It was the first indication I had had since we left Canada eleven days ago that I might play in Moscow. But how could I play? I had played so poorly in Canada. I was bewildered. At the end of practice, Harry skated over to me and said that I'd start tomorrow night. I had not played a game in more than two weeks. Here I was with a zero and three record against the Russians and an astronomical goals-against average of seven per game. It did not make sense. And Tony, of course, played very well Friday night even though we lost the game. If Harry changed, I thought he'd switch to E. J.

After practice, Lynda and I toured the Kremlin. We walked through the main gate and past the Palace of Congresses to an enormous theater — supposedly the biggest in the world — made out of white marble. It provided a stark contrast to most of the old, yellow buildings inside the Kremlin. We saw a huge cannon that Peter the Great had built but never fired because it was too big and heavy for his soldiers. Then we

[125]

At the right moment defenseman Pat Stapleton pokes the puck from Aleksander Yakushev (15) in Vancouver during our last Canadian game.

strolled into an armorylike building which houses the jewels and other valuable possessions of all the Russian czars.

Back at the hotel I had to laugh at the last paragraph of the game story in *Sovetsky Sport*. "The Soviet team," someone named V. Yurzinov wrote, "showed its character and won a valuable victory. But doing justice to our players, we would like to ask them not to make their hockey fans so nervous, to start playing not in the third period Sunday night but right from the beginning." I wanted to sleep for an hour so I wouldn't sleep tonight during one of Tchaikovsky's operas at the Palace of Congresses. But I was dead tired, fighting my cold, and instead of sleeping for just an hour I slept through the night.

September 24

Ever feel so nervous, so on edge that you almost can't stand up? That's the way I feel right now — and it's only quarter to nine in the morning, still eleven hours away from game time. I haven't felt this shaky since the first time I played the Russians three years ago in Vancouver. Then I was the definite second goalie, behind Wayne Stephanson of the Canadian National Team, and was getting one chance to prove whether or not I was any good. The fear of failure is wicked. I did not have any such feelings, however, the night before my first Stanley Cup game against Boston in 1971. After all, I had played six NHL games at the end of the regular season and we had won all six. But my record against the Russians. . . . Well, let's not talk about it.

I wonder how the other players feel about Harry's decision to play me again. I'm sure they think Tony should be playing tonight, and I can't really blame them. In fact, I sensed that feeling yesterday after practice. You know, I have not given them many reasons to believe that all of a sudden I'll play well against the Russians. But now that I think about it, there are a few reasons why I might. My reasons:

1) I was rusty in Canada but now I have two games and a month of practice under my belt.

2) I have changed my style to accommodate the strong points of the Soviet game. Mentally, at least, this seems to have caused a big improvement in my performances. Although I still have not tried the new style in a game, I have developed a quiet confidence in it. At first it *was* new and I didn't know if I could play that way or indeed if it was the right way. Now I'm certain; so certain, in fact, that I know that under pressure I will not revert back to the old Dryden style.

3) The team is playing much better.

I spent all day in a thorough soul- and mind-searching session. At the morning meeting at the rink, Harry noted that the Russians had improved noticeably on the face-offs and that our centers will have to concentrate a little better during the draws. In Canada we probably won seventy-five percent of the face-offs; in the first game here in Moscow we won less than fifty percent. One other thing: Gilbert Perreault has returned to Canada. He scored a big goal in Vancouver, then set up an important goal here in the game Friday night. But he said he was not playing enough. So Pat Stapleton approached Harry and told him, "Here I come to Moscow for a vacation and end up playing all the games!" He was joking, of course.

The quality of our meals has gone down. The great initial burst of big steaks has become a retreat to mini-steaks. We never get Cokes, though they are talked about all the time. But I guess what we're getting to eat is better than what our wives are being served. In fact, Lynda and some other wives came to the door at lunch and asked for handouts.

One thing the Canadian fans seem to be doing well — besides keeping the dollar bars open until the wee hours and marching through Red Square with their little Canadian flags — is providing some cheer to the normally drab Moscow scene. They all wear those round "smile" stickers on their lapels and pocketbooks and hats. Some fan even pasted them on all the doors on the ninth floor of the Intourist.

The fans back home have sent thousands of telegrams, and we have papered the walls of the dressing rooms at the rink with their messages of good cheer. For instance, one telegram from Moncton, New Brunswick, has at least one thousand names on it, and there are more than four thousand names on a wire from Simcoe, Ontario. Remarkable. And quite a boost. Probably half the people in Sault Sainte Marie, Ontario, have signed the telegrams addressed to the Esposito brothers. "Hey, Phil," Tony said this morning as he read the names of his neighbors, "I didn't know that Frank Donatelli married that girl what's her name." Phil didn't know, either.

In the room before the game, it was obvious that we were all aware of the importance of the sixth game. If we lost, the series was lost. A tie might produce an eventual tie in the series, but a tie was also a loss. Almost overnight a number of minor injuries had cropped up, too. Bill White's hand was sore, Pat Stapleton was having trouble with an old pulled muscle, and Gary Bergman was having muscle spasms in his back. No way they'll miss this game, though, if I know them.

Most of the other players sensed I was psychologically

up for the game, but maybe not psyched-up enough because of my previous experiences against the Russians. So they went to work on me. "C'mon, you're the best," they said. "Play your best. Stand 'em on their ears." It was really encouraging, almost to the point of making me too nervous. Yet it was embarrassing to know that they knew I needed the encouragement. In the pregame warmup, every time I stopped a shot — even the easiest ones — fifteen guys would yell out, "Way to go, big guy, way to go. . . . Cripes, we can't get a pea past ya. . . . Boy, you got it tonight." On and on it went, and after a time it really became a bit funny.

Confidence is a valuable tool, particularly for a goaltender. For instance, if a goalie makes a couple of tough saves early in a game, it seems to inspire not only the goaltender but also his teammates. However, if a goalie looks bad at the start of a game and gives up a couple of easy goals, well, psychologically his teammates get depressed because they figure they will have to score an inordinate number of goals to outscore the opposition.

The Russians roared out for the first period, and in the early moments I made three really good saves. Each time I stopped the puck, I had a feeling of accomplishment. I also became more confident, more and more at home. We had to play shorthanded for almost six straight minutes right after the midway point of the first period, but again I made some good saves on tough shots. I *was* staying in my net, and I *was* moving fast enough to pick off the close-in shots without great problems. I also was a bit lucky late in the period when Kharlamov — perched at the corner of the crease — hit the goalpost when he had about half the net staring at him.

Early in the second period the Russians scored when Yuri Liapkin fired a low shot from the blue line that tipped off the back of someone's skate and flew into the far corner, just past my glove. Then suddenly we came back ourselves and scored three goals within eighty-three seconds. First it was Dennis Hull banging a loose puck under Tretiak. Then it was Cournoyer slapping in a rebound. And finally it was Paul Henderson, intercepting a clearing pass at the blue line, taking two long strides, and then firing a bouncing forty-footer past Tretiak's left foot. Now we led 3–1.

I can't explain what happened next. We had the game under control. We were up two goals, we had momentum, and we remembered what had happened two nights before: five Russian goals in the third period. All we had to do was play smart, positional, close-checking hockey. For some reason, though, we didn't. We played stupidly. We began to get penalties and penalties and more penalties. In fact, all in all the two West German referees gave *us* twenty-nine minutes in penalties and only four minutes to the Russians.

So suddenly it was 3–2, as Yakushev scored on another power play late in the second period. And more trouble was on the way. Half a minute later Phil Esposito took a five-minute penalty for cutting Ragulin with a high stick in the corner, and at the same time the referees added on a two-minute bench penalty for something Fergy said to them. Geez Murphy. They came at us in brigades, but our defensemen, particularly Serge Savard (who had cracked his ankle only seventeen days before in Winnipeg), repeatedly broke up their passing plays near the net.

Once I thought the Russians scored. I think they thought they had scored, too. But the red light never went on. Yakushev was on my right and he passed the puck across the goal mouth to Kharlamov, who was standing at the corner of the crease. I felt helpless as I moved over to try and stop Kharlamov's shot. The puck hit my pad and caromed towards the net. What happened next I don't know. The puck could have hit the goalpost and flown back to me. Or it could have hit the mesh netting inside the net and flown back. All I knew was that the puck was in my glove and the referee was whistling the play dead.

Thank goodness the period ended a few seconds later. In the room we dressed ourselves down pretty severely. We realized we were losing control of our emotions and the game. Despite everything, though, we were ahead. Harry told us: "Let's concentrate and win the game." For psychological reasons he also kept us in the dressing room an extra five minutes before the start of the third period. More rest for the weary.

We could not have played a better third period. The Russians did not challenge us because we never let them. We didn't score ourselves, but we were always in control, until the last two minutes of the period when Ron Ellis took a holding penalty. Trouble. Liapkin almost scored through a screen — but the puck bounced off the edge of my pads. Then Lutchenko almost caught the corner from twenty-five feet, but the puck deflected off my glove. The last gasp!

It was over. We had rallied. We had won 3–2. I finally beat the Russians. It sounds like a cliché, but I felt that the weight of the world had been lifted from my back. I know I was not a popular choice among the players, the press and the Canadian fans before the game. Indeed, Harry and Fergy would have been subjected to considerable criticism if I had played a bad game. They certainly took a big gamble on me. I had not given them any indication that I would play well. Lynda told me that a fan sitting near her in the stands called Sinden a "jerk" for "playing that idiot Dryden." But it was all over — and what a relief.

It was a happy time in the dressing room, and I thanked all the guys for being so encouraging before the game. We are back now. Sure, we are not favorites to win the series — we're still down 3–2–1 after six games — but we have a chance.

I met Lynda and my father back at the hotel. Lynda said she was exhausted. "What are you tired about?" I said to her. She gave me a dirty look. "Listen, buster," she said, "if you knew what I went through tonight you'd be tired, too."

September 25

Practice. A happy practice for a change. Harry and Fergy and Al Eagleson came out to the rink early for a meeting with the Soviet hockey people about the West German referees — Joseph Kompalla and Franz Baader — who had worked last night. After the game Harry called them "the most incompetent officials I've ever seen." Now we want the Russians to reciprocate for our favor in Winnipeg, when the Russians protested the work of the officials in the second game. In fact, Eagleson flat-out says we won't play the eighth game if the Russians exercise their prerogative and select Kompalla and Baader as the officials.

At practice Harry said that Tony would play the seventh game tomorrow night and that I'd play the eighth game regardless of the situation. Later on, I took a couple of pucks and fired them into the net from the spot where Kharlamov apparently missed that sure goal last night. The netting *is* pretty tight there. A puck could boomerang in and out in a fraction of a second.

Bobrov, the Soviet coach, even suggested in an interview with *Sovetsky Sport* that Kharlamov did indeed put the puck into the net. In the interview he stressed how the Russians controlled themselves with respect to debating the officials and used the Kharlamov nongoal as an example. Possibly he is right. The Russians certainly did not protest at the time. They questioned in a minor way, quietly asking the referee if the puck went in, but when he said no they quickly dropped the subject. Now, if the same thing had happened in North America, I suspect that the reaction would have been a bit more vehement. Someone certainly would have whacked a stick against the glass in front of the goal judge's seat, at the very least.

Again, the Soviet newspapers murdered us. B. Fedosov, writing in *Izvestia*, said:

> The Canadians were openly hunting after Kharlamov. This apology for hockey is alien to us and this is why our sportsmen did not hit back either in Toronto or in Moscow. Phil Esposito was especially rude. If rudeness is a tactical principle of Canadian professionals, then this undermines the essence of sports competition and may make it impossible.

One other thing we read every day is the promotion about the remarkable showing of the Communist bloc at the Olympics in Munich. As every Canadian here in Moscow knows by now, the athletes of eleven socialist countries accounted for barely ten percent of the participants in the Olympics yet won forty-eight percent of the medals (285). And Vitaly Smirnov, the first-deputy chairman of the Soviet Committee for Physical Culture and Sport, boasted: "The success of the Soviet

Stan Mikita (fingers to his lips) and Bobby Orr watch the action from the stands. So that's where our power play was.

teams is based on the solid foundation of participation of millions in sports activities in the USSR."

The Russians estimate they have more than six hundred thousand senior amateur players and more than three million youngsters registered in various hockey programs. "I cannot give you an exact figure on the kids," Kirill Romensky of the Hockey Federation says, "because it is difficult to keep track. In Siberia, you know, they start to skate the minute they get out of the napkin." Maybe so. But let's see how the system works, using Tretiak as an example.

Like all Russian youths, Tretiak, who was born in Moscow twenty years ago, began to attend state-sponsored sports classes when he turned seven. For the next three years he worked at many sports, hockey, volleyball, basketball, soccer, ski jumping, gymnastics, tennis and began to develop his physique under the watchful eyes of special training instructors, all graduates of physical culture institutes. Besides teaching Tretiak the strict, state-approved way of, say, shooting free throws, these instructors also tested his mental and psychological qualities. Their appraisals were then forwarded to the Committee for Sports and Moscow's Physical Culture Research Institute for official examination. Tretiak obviously possessed all the traits of the perfect goaltender, so at the age of eleven he was given some armor and told to become the new Jacques Plante. At this point, he was separated from most of his peers and placed in a junior sports school at the Central Army Club in Moscow. There are only three standard indoor rinks in Moscow, including the Army Club arena, and only selected youths such as Tretiak ever get to play on them. The club is also one of the top training grounds for Russia's best athletes.

Now compare this with the normal procedure for finding goaltenders in North America. As a rule, a kid becomes a goaltender because he can't skate well enough to be a forward or has a stocky frame or happens to have an old pair of goalie pads that his grandfather gave his father thirty years ago. There is no scientific method for mating an athlete and a particular position as there is in Russia.

In time, Tretiak became the best young goaltender in Russia, and at the age of fifteen he came under the expert tutelage of Anatoli Tarasov, who was the National Team's coach at the time and also the head coach of the Central Army Club. Tarasov spent hours every day with Tretiak, drilling him on the finer points of goaltending as he himself had learned them from the Canadians. Tretiak was now a member of Russia's young elite, someone who would not be spending the rest of his days manning a lathe somewhere. One of the attractions of sport in Russia is that it is the fastest way out of the gray-black anonymity and into the world of wash-and-wear shirts, automobiles and two-bedroom apartments.

Tretiak continued to improve, and in 1970 Tarasov considered him ready not only for the Central Army team in Russia's major hockey league but also for the National Team in world competition. But Tretiak had to find permanent employment, because the Russians insist that their players are unpaid amateurs, and any jobless individual in the Soviet Union may be arrested on a charge of parasitism. No problem. He was made a private in the Soviet army and assigned the task of developing another Tretiak. Earlier this month, probably as the direct result of his performances in Canada, Private Tretiak was promoted overnight to Lieutenant Tretiak. As a lieutenant-goaltender assigned to the Central Army Club, Tretiak's salary is more than four hundred rubles (about five hundred dollars) a month. But like the other Soviet hockey players, he also earns sizable bonuses for outstanding athletic accomplishments, such as winning Olympic gold medals and victories over Canadian professionals. His bonus for this series will be as much as two thousand rubles if the Russians win, somewhat less if they lose.

Like all the other players on the National Team, Tretiak works at hockey eleven months of the year and takes a couple of weeks' vacation, usually during June, at the Central Army Club resort on the Black Sea.

I drove over to see the Army Club this afternoon with Jack Ludwig, a former professor at the State University of New York at Stony Brook and now a free-lance writer in Canada. It is located on the west side of Moscow, and you have to pass through a big gate to get onto the grounds. The club has so many facilities it makes the normal Y look unfurnished. The Army Club has large, separate buildings for hockey, tennis, weight lifting, swimming, gymnastics and basketball, as well as a seven-thousand-seat soccer stadium. Between the buildings are outdoor basketball courts, volleyball grounds and mini-sized soccer fields. In the hockey arena there is also a special rink strictly for figure skaters; later, I saw two dozen petite Russian girls, all about seven years old, practicing their splits and jumps under the steely supervision of their coach.

It was raining outside as we walked around the grounds, but nevertheless a couple of Russian hockey coaches — decked out in the traditional royal blue sweat suit with the white stripe down the sides — were putting their young players through exercise drills. There were perhaps thirty boys in all, about ten or eleven years old. The coach, who also went through the exercises, was a man named Brezhnev, no relation to the Communist party boss, and in the late fifties and early sixties he had been a defenseman on the National Team. Now, he told me, he is a junior coach at the Army Club.

I asked one of the youngsters, a boy named Vyacheslav, who his favorite player was. "It is Boris Mikhailov, of course," he said. "He is a gentleman." I asked him how he liked Kharlamov, who would be the darling of most North American fans because of his electric skating style and lightning-fast moves. Vyacheslav shook his head. "Kharlamov is a witch," he said, frowning. "He is a fast skater. But Boris Mikhailov, he is a gentleman." I don't think it's any coincidence that Vyacheslav's favorite — Mikhailov — is pursuing a master's degree in engineering, while Kharlamov is more or less a hockey player only. "Someone like Mikhailov is held up to these boys as the highest product of the system," my interpreter said, "and the youngsters are urged to become Mikhailovs themselves."

The outdoor drills were very intriguing. First of all, it was obvious that the kids were having a good time. The coaches did not try to present the exercises to the boys in a heavy-handed manner, and there seemed to be a great rapport between them and the players. When is the last time you saw kids in North America enjoying push-ups and sit-ups and body twists?

The exercises were seemingly unimportant drills, performed with no apparent goal. Keeping their hockey sticks in their hands, the boys hopped up onto a bench with one foot, then another, for several minutes, then engaged in some forty-yard foot races. Later, they did shoulder rolls and somersaults into a sawdust pit. The scene resembled the obstacle course at a training center for military inductees in the United States. A while later, Brezhnev tossed three dozen tennis balls onto a court and the boys had to stickhandle among one another for eight or ten minutes. Try that sometime; it's very difficult. But it teaches you to keep your head up — or else.

The ultimate goal of these drills was to improve the agility and the balance of the players. The premise that the Russians work on is this: the better an all-round athlete you can make a youngster, the better a performer he eventually will be. So, rather than teach a certain skill in a certain sport, they develop the complete athlete. A sound premise, I'd say. The good athlete can always pick up specific skills for a specific sport. I'm sure that Bobby Orr could learn to hit a curve ball, and that Johnny Bench could learn to stop a hockey puck.

After watching the kids, I went inside to see the regular drills. The rink itself was a duplicate of the typical rink in a small Canadian city, with a low ceiling and only about twelve or fifteen rows of benches on both sides of the ice. But the ice itself was good — not too soft or too slow — and that is really all that counts. There were more than forty youngsters on the ice at one time, and while the general sight looked fairly confusing, the more I looked, the more I realized that the kids had been organized into different groups and were doing completely different drills. Not once during the hour or so that I watched the workout did the players from one group interfere with the players from another. But what I liked most was that all the players seemed to be doing something.

The main coach conducting the drill was B. Vinogradov, also a former player with the National Team. He had a number of subordinate coaches handling the particular drills for the different groups. Vinogradov worked with a microphone from a bench at one side of the rink as the overseer. It hit me that he could be compared to Bear Bryant, Darrell Royal, and every other college football coach with fifteen assistants.

Typically, Vinogradov's drills — or the state's drills —

were intended primarily as agility exercises. Dribbling a puck, the players would skate to the blue line, fall onto their knees while still controlling the puck, then jump up and skate to the next blue line and repeat the fall onto the ice. Later, Vinogradov threw about forty pucks onto center ice and all the players had to stickhandle within the blue lines. Again, you learn to keep your head up. At the end of the two-hour session Vinogradov put the players through a long skating exercise. Down and back. Down and back. Down and back. Stop and start. Stop and start. But it was not that simple. While the players were skating furiously, the coaches went around and attempted to throw body checks. So the players had to keep their heads up or else they got knocked onto the ice. And they also learned to develop enough agility so they could avoid body checks while in full flight. Very interesting.

The equipment the young players had was poor by Canadian standards, although it was not really bad. Old, perhaps, but adequate. Superior by Russian standards. The lack of new seventy-five-dollar skates and new fifty-dollar gloves did not seem to bother the kids as far as protection and comfort were concerned.

Later on, Boris Kulagin, the No. 2 coach of the National Team, showed up with about fifteen players, most of whom were with the Nationals but had not played in many of the games in the series so far. For thirty minutes these players worked on their passing, stickhandling, shooting and breakout plays, then they scrimmaged for a solid hour. Nonstop. No substitutions. All the while, Kulagin stood against the boards with a microphone in his hand and barked pertinent comments as the players swirled about.

"*Bystree, bystree!*" he shouted. "Faster, faster! You can do nothing without moving!" One of the players made a bad pass, then fell down and took his time getting up. "*Shto ty delayesh?*" Kulagin screamed angrily into the microphone. "What are you doing?" Later, one of the players tried a solo down the ice and was easily stopped. Kulagin shook his head and waved at the guilty individual. "Can't you count to two?" he said, meaning that the player had better pass to another player next time — or else.

When Harry Sinden was told how Kulagin used the microphone, he just shook his head. "Why couldn't we think of using a mike on the ice? No, we have to yell at the players, and they either can't hear or don't want to hear us."

As I think about it now, it's pretty easy to understand how Tretiak has developed into such an excellent goaltender. The Soviet coaches commit themselves totally to the involved teaching process that most North American coaches prefer to shun. For instance, last year Tretiak had what Stanislas Kashta, the coach of the Czechoslovakian National Team, called "the worst glove hand in the world." Now his glove hand is quicker than any of our shooters ever dreamed. What happened? "He learned to use his glove hand during the summer," Kulagin said. After every workout with the National Team, Kulagin and Bobrov kept Tretiak on the ice for at least another hour and forced him to face the firing squad: a shooting machine that fires a puck every four seconds at speeds up to one hundred miles an hour. Tretiak now may have one of the fastest gloves in the world.

I also think that the rigid Soviet training program has considerable merit. The National Team gathered on July 5 to begin formal workouts for this series — some six weeks before we met for the first time in Toronto. For the first four or five days, though, Bobrov and Kulagin did not permit their players to go onto the ice.

"Physical fitness, psychological fitness and courage combine with technical ability to make skill," Bobrov says. "We work on the first three parts, then think about the technical part." Each day the Russians started their training on a basketball court. "A little basketball is good for the reflexes," Kulagin says. Yes, and good for perfecting the interference play, too.

Then came medicine balls, weight lifting, soccer and gymnastics. Finally, some hockey on a hardwood floor. The forwards and the defensemen passed weighted pucks with lead hockey sticks. "When at last they get onto the ice," Bobrov says, "the regular sticks and pucks feel like nothing to them." Meanwhile, off in a corner, Tretiak and the other goaltenders used one hand to stickhandle a weighted puck with their lead goalie's stick; with the other hand they repeatedly flipped a ball in and out of their goalie's glove. "Very good for hand-eye coordination," Bobrov says. The Soviet players also took physical and psychological tests, and only those who passed remained on the team.

Here is the basic schedule that the Russians followed during their training-camp period of preparation for the series against Canada:

DATE	HOURS	PROGRAM	
July 5	11:30–13:50	Workout Gymnastics Soccer Run	2 hrs. 20 mins.
July 6	11:00–13:00	Workout Gymnastics Acrobatics Basketball	2 hrs.
July 7	10:00–12:00	Workout Gymnastics Track and field Soccer	2 hrs.

DATE	HOURS	PROGRAM	
July 8	10:00–10:45	Workout	2 hrs.
	11:45–13:00	Technical-tactical preparation	
July 9	11:00–14:00	Workout on ice	3 hrs.

TOTAL IN ONE WEEK: 11 hours 20 minutes

July 11	10:00–10:45	Workout	
	11:15–13:00	Technical-tactical preparation on ice	4 hrs. 30 mins.
	17:00–19:00	Individual practice on ice	
July 12	10:00–10:45	Workout	
	11:15–13:00	Technical-tactical preparation on ice	4 hrs. 30 mins.
	17:00–19:00	Game	
July 13	9:00–10:00	Individual preparation on ice	1 hr.
	11:00–13:00	Bath, massage	
July 14	10:00–10:45	Workout	
	11:15–13:00	Technical-tactical preparation on ice	2 hrs. 30 mins.
July 15	10:00–10:45	Workout	
	11:15–13:00	Technical-tactical preparation on ice	4 hrs. 30 mins.
	17:00–19:00	Game	
July 16	10:00–10:45	Workout	
	11:45–13:00	Technical-tactical preparation on ice	2 hrs.

TOTAL IN ONE WEEK: 19 hours

July 18	10:00–10:45	Workout	
	11:00–13:00	Technical-tactical preparation on ice	4 hrs. 45 mins.
	18:00–20:00	Workout	
July 19	8:30–9:30	Morning gymnastics	
	12:00–14:00	Workout	5 hrs.
	18:00–20:00	Soccer	

DATE	HOURS	PROGRAM	
July 20	8:30–9:30	Morning gymnastics	
	11:00–13:30	Workout on ice	3 hrs. 30 mins.
July 21	17:00–18:00	Hockey theory	
	18:30–20:30	Game	2 hrs.
July 22	10:00–10:45	Workout	
	11:00–13:00	Technical-tactical preparation on ice	2 hrs. 45 mins.
	17:00–19:00	Hockey theory	
July 23	8:30–9:30	Morning gymnastics	
	11:00–13:30	Technical-tactical preparation on ice	3 hrs. 30 mins.
		Workout on ice	

TOTAL IN ONE WEEK: 21 hours 30 minutes

July 25	10:00–10:45	Workout	
	11:00–13:00	Technical-tactical preparation on ice	2 hrs. 45 mins.
July 26	8:30–9:30	Morning gymnastics	
	11:00–12:30	Hockey theory	
	12:45–14:00	Individual practice on ice (goalies)	4 hrs. 45 mins.
	18:30–20:30	Game	
July 27	9:00–10:00	Individual practice on ice	1 hr.
	11:00–13:00	Bath, massage	
July 28	10:00–10:45	Workout	
	11:00–13:00	Technical-tactical preparation on ice	2 hrs. 45 mins.
July 29	8:30–9:30	Morning gymnastics	
	10:00–12:30	Cross-country run	5 hrs. 30 mins.
	18:00–20:00	Soccer	
July 30	8:30–9:30	Morning gymnastics	3 hrs.
	11:00–13:00	Technical-tactical preparation on ice	

TOTAL IN ONE WEEK: 19 hours 45 minutes

DATE	HOURS	PROGRAM	
Aug. 1	10:00–10:45	Workout	
	11:00–13:00	Technical-tactical preparation on ice	2 hrs. 45 mins.
Aug. 2	10:00–10:45	Workout	
	11:00–13:00	Technical-tactical preparation on ice	4 hrs. 45 mins.
	17:00–19:00	Game	
Aug. 3	9:00–10:00	Individual practice on ice	1 hr.
	10:00–13:00	Bath, massage	
Aug. 4	15:00–15:45	Workout	
	16:00–18:00	Technical-tactical preparation on ice	2 hrs. 45 mins.
Aug. 5	8:30–9:30	Morning gymnastics	
	11:00–12:00	Workout	4 hrs.
	18:00–20:00	Soccer	
Aug. 6	8:30–9:00	Morning gymnastics	
	11:00–12:00	Individual workout	4 hrs. 30 mins.
	12:00–13:00	Preparation for game (individual training)	
	16:30–18:30	Game	

TOTAL IN ONE WEEK: 19 hours 45 minutes

DATE	HOURS	PROGRAM	
Aug. 8	10:00–10:45	Workout	
	11:00–13:00	Technical-tactical preparation on ice	2 hrs. 45 mins.
Aug. 9	10:00–10:45	Workout	
	11:00–13:00	Technical-tactical preparation on ice	2 hrs. 45 mins.
Aug. 10	9:00–10:00	Individual training on ice	1 hr.
	11:00–13:00	Bath, massage	
Aug. 11	8:30–9:30	Morning gymnastics	
	11:00–13:00	Workout on ice	5 hrs.
	17:00–19:00	Game	

DATE	HOURS	PROGRAM	
Aug. 12	8:30–9:30	Morning gymnastics	
	11:00–12:00	Individual training on ice	4 hrs.
	17:00–19:00	Game	
Aug. 13	8:30–9:30	Morning gymnastics	
	11:00–12:00	Individual workout	4 hrs.
	16:30–18:30	Game	

TOTAL IN ONE WEEK: 19 hours 30 mins.

Before leaving the Army Club, I also talked to some Russian coaches about the major hockey league in the Soviet Union, the NHL of Russia. There are nine teams in the league, and all are supported by various trade unions or factories or army clubs, not by the state as such. For instance, Spartak, the most popular team among the fans because of its hell-for-leather playing style, represents a cooperative of light industries. Dynamo is sponsored by the police and the KGB (sort of Moscow's FBI). Krylya Soviet (the Wings of the Soviet), a team of the league's youngest players coached by Kulagin, represents some trade unions in Moscow. There also is the Leningrad Army Club, Torpedo of Gorki (a car and truck plant), Khimik (a chemistry plant), Traktor of Siberia (a tractor plant), and Lokomotiv of Moscow (an engine factory), as well as the Moscow Central Army Club.

Games involving the Central Army Club, Dynamo and Spartak always sell out the Palace of Sport (the top ticket price is less than two dollars), but when Traktor comes from Siberia to play Lokomotiv, there are empty seats everywhere. The league plays a thirty-two-game schedule, and the Central Army Club, now coached by Tarasov, has won the regular-season championship nine times in the last ten years. No wonder. Most of the National Team players also skate for the Central Army Club.

As we were leaving, Kulagin offered his own explanation for the fast development of Russian hockey players. "The Canadians," he said simply, "are not as serious about hockey as we are. Everything in hockey is in the seriousness of the approach." Despite everything, though, I can't see hockey becoming an eleven-months-a-year job for our professionals. In the Soviet Union, many players automatically qualify for coaching jobs at the end of their career and have no problem finding good employment. Canadian pros, however, if forced to play eight hours a day, eleven months of the year, would not have the opportunity to train themselves for postathletic careers.

We are simply a different people entirely; I don't foresee any change. We have a class system, with stars of various magnitude while the Russians follow the socialist system and attempt to play down what they call our "cult of personality." In Russia there are no postgame television shows, no star-of-the-game shows, no locker-room interviews for the afternoon papers, no endorsements of automobiles or clothes or shaving cream. In commenting about a game, Bobrov and Kulagin never say, "Tretiak was very good." Instead, they make only the very general comment that "the goaltender was good." The goaltender! Not Tretiak, the goaltender. No, I can't see North Americans suddenly downplaying the personality cult and the star syndrome now.

It was dinner time when I got back to the hotel, and after dinner we all had to rush off to a cocktail party at the Canadian embassy. After that we dashed to the Palace of Congresses to see a variety show put on by the Bolshoi. The first half of the show consisted of comedians and classical singers as well as a few dramatic readings

Gilbert Perreault fends off
Aleksander Yakushev as
Tony Esposito awaits a shot
that is sure to come.

of poetry, and despite the language barrier, it was very good. The second half was a songfest with six male singers playing different instruments, and not nearly as good. Apparently they are Russia's answer to the Rolling Stones, but they played and sang more like the Andrews Sisters.

September 26

I worked out for an hour this morning with the Black Aces so I could stay sharp for the eighth game on Thursday night. Tony, of course, will be playing tonight, and E. J. will be the backup goalie. After the workout I went over to the Institute of Sports and Physical Culture, the nerve center for Soviet sports. It is located in an old building that was once the residence of some famous Russian count. The building is in bad disrepair, but a new one already has been built across town, where the workmen are still adding some final touches.

Entering the building, I walked down a long hallway that had various detailed medical charts encased on the side walls. The charts showed not only bones and muscles but also nerves and blood vessels for every part of the body. I have no background at all in biology or anatomy, so the charts and graphs meant little to me. Still, it hit me that whoever uses these things — like the future players and the future instructors — certainly will benefit from them. The Soviet athletic system emphasizes that you must know the limits and potentials of your own body. By knowing where an injury is and what effect it will have on your performance, by being able to semi-diagnose your injury before the doctor does, you can determine not only how serious it is but whether you can continue to perform with it. By knowing your body well you can better inform the doctor where the injury and the pain really are located.

Beyond that first corridor there was another corridor with another series of glass encasements on the wall. This time, though, they contained wooden-box mock-ups of the various bones, ligaments and muscles, as well as the joints, the muscle and the skull points. They were ultragraphic, you might say. It was intriguing to see the exact physical structure of the knee. For twenty years now I have been reading about torn ligaments and torn cartilages without really understanding what they were. Now, the next time someone gets such an injury I will at least be able to comprehend what has happened. By looking at the structure of the knee, it also became very obvious why there are so many knee injuries.

At the end of the second corridor we noticed some of the instructors. One of them spoke a few words of English and sort of understood us when we told him who we were. Then that person left and in a few minutes came back with his sister, a lady named Helen Anisinova who spoke excellent English and agreed to play interpreter for us. She took us through the main office complex of the institute and then into the office of the director. In the room with him were five instructors, including a former star of the Soviet National Soccer Team. For the next two hours we peppered them with countless questions, and they were more than willing to answer all of them.

We found out there are nine similar institutes in the Soviet Union, with many others at different levels of complexity. The institute here is considered a high-level training complex; another one outside the city, where Tretiak is among the students, is considered inter-mediate-level. Basically, the institutes instruct current athletes, former athletes and other interested people in the art of coaching. Besides learning the technical points involved in their particular sport, the prospective instructors also learn about anatomy, physiology, and psychology, as well as the history of their sport and its position in society.

These prospective coaches attend the institute ten hours a week for five years. Four of the hours are devoted to theory and the nontechnical aspects of sport; the other six hours are practical teaching. For instance, the instructors break down the mechanics of shooting, passing, and goaltending. They will, for example, demonstrate that unless your thumb sets comfortably on the stick you can't possibly expect to get off a hard shot. They also talk about oxygen intake, lung capacity and many other such topics that most coaches in North America undoubtedly have never heard about. In other words, what the Russians do so well is tap all the available resources and make the perfect, rounded coach. Really, there is not just one Tarasov and one Bobrov and one Kulagin in the Soviet Union — but many.

Thinking about this, I must dispute the charge that once sport is made scientific it no longer is sport. That's stupid thinking. Sport is much more than just the naked physicality of competition. It *does* involve the mind as well as the body; it not only does but it should. Sport, to me, should develop the entire person. The philosophy of sport seems antiquated in North America, while the Russians have modernized everything. Their coaches and athletes understand the reasons for doing things. Over here, we are told to do something, and we do it, without any explanation of the purpose. All in all, it seems pretty logical that the more you know about your body, and the more you know about playing your sport, then the better person and the better athlete you will be.

I asked one of the instructors what he thought about

the Canadian hockey players. His response indicated, I think, the rapport we had established. He said we seemed like fine people and a fine team but he did not understand why we had to play so rudely. I'm glad he said it. It certainly was not a standard propaganda response. He asked me how I liked playing the Russians. I said that I honestly enjoyed playing against them but that I didn't enjoy playing against the chippy Swedes. I told him I always enjoy playing against teams and people who do things well.

Later, I asked another coach what the Russian players do besides play hockey. Many of them, he said, work in factories, many are in school and many are in the army. The active players who do attend the institute work for a degree on their own schedule because of the stiff demands of their hockey program. Besides the regular schedule of thirty-two games, the Russian Nationals play another fifty or so games in international competition.

Well, I said, how long does it take the average hockey player to complete the institute?

"Twenty-five years," an instructor said.

I looked puzzled. All the Russians laughed. My interpreter said, "It's a joke." Then I laughed, too.

What the instructor meant, of course, was that hockey players are looked upon as "jocks" in the Soviet system. Sort of like the jocks who play big-time college football in the United States and never have time to complete their schooling. Actually, the average Soviet hockey player completes the institute in about seven and one-half years.

What is interesting about the institute is that the Soviets don't let their athletes become just athletes. Their philosophy obviously is to round out the athlete and make him a useful vehicle once his playing days are over. Interesting. Our concept of the Soviet player, of course, is that he is more professional than the North American professional, because he spends forty-eight weeks a year in training. To some degree that is true, but he does not involve himself only with active sports. Take Vyacheslav Starshinov and Vladimir Shadrin, two of the older Russian players. Starshinov is an engineer pursuing his doctorate, while Shadrin teaches mathematics at Moscow University.

One of the instructors asked me if I thought my height was beneficial in the goal. He obviously felt that I was too tall; by the Russian computer I probably would have become a basketball player, not a goalie. I told him that as far as the goaltender is concerned, an apparent excess — like my 6 feet 4 inches — tends to balance an apparent lack of mobility. They cancel each other out.

I spent four hours at the institute and before leaving took some pictures of the instructors. The long session proved wrong the traditional notion that when you talk to people involved with Soviet sports they tend to give you not answers but the state-approved and state-taught propaganda. Sort of the double-talk shuffle. But it was not that way at the institute, where the people could not have been more accommodating. Sometime I'd like to spend a month or two there and participate in the curriculum. We should study their techniques and method, for it is the prime area where we in North America have been totally backward.

We do have a lot to learn.

On the way to the game at the Palace of Sport, I talked with Dr. Jim Murray about my visit to the institute. He said he had spent the day at an athletic hospital in Moscow, a huge place of more than two thousand beds used only for the treatment of athletic injuries. Ballet dancers and circus performers are considered athletes, so in other words it really is a status hospital for performers. If a soccer player tears the ligaments in his knee during a game five thousand miles away in Vladivostok, they fly him right back to Moscow and rush him to the special hospital. Dr. Murray said he didn't think Soviet medicine was as advanced or as sophisticated as North American medicine. But he said their general standard of care is more advanced, because they seem to have more doctors and nurses and aides than the hospitals in North America.

At the rink, the Canadian fans seemed noisier than ever. They had coined a new chant — "da da Canada, nyet nyet Soviet" — and the din was terrific. For some reason — maybe because of the high decibel count — the Russian militiamen confiscated all the Canadian air horns at the gates, but that didn't seem to stop our inventive fans. One man taped the incessant blowing of an air horn on his recorder and had no trouble smuggling it in under his coat. So the militiamen understandably went into a rage when they heard the noise of an air horn.

Harry did not have to say very much in the dressing room. All the players knew how important this game was, so there was a hush in the air. Gary Bergman will have to maintain his silence during the game, too. Harry reached an agreement with the Russians over the selection of the officials for the eighth game Thursday night: they say they will not use the West German officials — Kompalla and Baader — if Bergman promises not to yell insults at Bobrov every time he skates past the Russian bench. Poor Gary. Harry and Fergy may gag him.

At the start, play was sluggish. Neither team seemed ready to play well; in fact, if either team had started well, the other side would have been in desperate shape. I watched from the stands with Don Awrey, and now I know one of the reasons they call him Bugsy. He can't sit still for a fraction of a second. Worse yet, he's a body checker as he watches a game; he gets so wrapped up with the flow of play that he throws elbows and kicks his feet and thrusts his shoulders in every direction. I'm sure I'll wake up with some sore bones tomorrow.

As rough as it was sitting next to Bugsy in the stands, though, it was worse out on the ice as the referees, Rudy Batja of Czechoslovakia and Uve Dahlberg of Sweden, had to call eighteen penalties — eleven on Canada and seven on Russia — to keep things under control. The game was for the most part what writers like to call a seesaw struggle. Phil Esposito scored early in the first period from you-know-where, but Yakushev — I'm really glad he won't be playing in the NHL — beat Tony from about thirty feet to tie the score after ten minutes. Bill White was in the penalty box for interference, of all things, as Petrov scored at 16:27, but Espo, after a neat pass from Serge Savard, beat Tretiak again to tie it at 17:34.

The second period was played mostly in the penalty box, then early in the third period Rod Gilbert surprised Tretiak when he came around from behind the net and stuck the puck between his legs for a goal. (The Canadian writers are now calling Rod "Mad Dog" because of the aggressive style he has displayed in Moscow; indeed, he's all over the place knocking guys down.) Then that man Yakushev — he may be the rich man's Mahovlich before this series is over — tied the score again on another power play.

As the clock ticked away, it looked certain that the game would end in a 3–3 tie. With three and one-half minutes to go, Boris Mikhailov and Gary Bergman went off after a pretty good fight in the corner, and after that the Russians went into a defensive pose. There were barely two minutes left to play as Savard got the puck in center ice and passed to Henderson, who was charging up ice.

Paul crossed the blue line, faked to his right, cut to his left — leaving Gennady Tsygankov, the defenseman, somewhere in Kiev or Leningrad — and bore down on Tretiak. As the goaltender went down, Henderson fired the puck over his right shoulder — just inside the post — and the red light went on. Henderson was sprawled on the ice, so was Tretiak. Paul got up first. Tony Esposito made a big save as we killed the last two minutes pretty well — and the series is all tied at 3–3–1.

I had mixed emotions as I walked towards the dressing room. I was happy that we had won, of course, but now I realized that we had to win the final game. And I would be playing goal. Wouldn't it be nice to live without that pressure the next two days! I was shook up, nervous, yet all the other Canadians were jubilant. They were even singing "Jingle Bells" because it was snowing outside. I could not share their jubilation at the time.

I went into the dressing room to congratulate the guys. Before I could speak, though, one of the players said to me, "You better be ready Thursday night, big guy." He meant it as a joke, and we both laughed, but the reminder was there: I *am* going to be in a tough spot two days from now. I walked out to meet Lynda. In my hand I was carrying a toy goaltender doll that the daughter of an Austrian embassy official had given to me before the game. Maybe if I wound up the doll it would stop the Russians Thursday night. I had better wind myself up, too.

Once again the Russian press has attacked us for what they now call our "uncovered crudity." I gather they mean our roughness, or at least what they think is roughness. One paper, *Sovetskaya Rossiya*, blames our "crudity" for the fact that defenseman Ragulin "got a trauma" and had to play with "a plaster" on his face. Kharlamov did not play last night because of an injury that resulted, the paper said, from "the real hunt the Canadian sportsmen arranged in the sixth game."

In describing the second period, when both teams made frequent visits to the penalty box, Viktor Sinyavsky wrote: "We can say the ice became larger. The point is that benches in the penalty box were not empty." What I liked best about the story, though, was his description of the Bergman-Mikhailov fight: "A few minutes before the game was over the Canadians commenced fighting. The referees made a strange decision: Bergman, who started fighting, left the ice — *and* Mikhailov." As I saw it, Mikhailov went into Bergman as Gary tried to freeze the puck against the boards and proceeded to kick Bergy in the back of the leg a couple of dozen times.

One thing Bobrov said surprised me. Talking about Henderson's winning goal, he commented: "Tsygankov cost us the game." *Not* "the defenseman cost us the game." "Tsygankov cost us the game." The team wins, but a player loses. Strange.

I tossed and turned most of the night, and at breakfast I still could not escape the pressure. Phil Esposito walked by and said, "Boy, you'd better be hot tomorrow night." He meant it good-naturedly — I knew that — but it was there nonetheless. No one ever seems to go to a defenseman or a forward and say: "You have to win it for us." They come to the goaltender. If the goaltender doesn't contribute, his team usually loses. A forward or a defenseman can have a bad night, though, and the team might win because some other forward or defenseman had a big night.

At practice my legs were rubbery, like two sponges, and my arms were tight. My mind was hopelessly boggled with thoughts about "tomorrow night." When will tomorrow night come so we can get it over with? I had to get away from it now. So I spent the rest of the day aimlessly wandering around Moscow with Lynda, Bob Lewis of *Time* Magazine, and an interpreter, a girl named Irina who had just become a mother a few weeks before. It was her first day back on the job. At first she was cool towards us, but gradually she became much friendlier.

She took us to a cemetery, the biggest one in Moscow. Cemetery! Just the place for me in my present frame of mind. She showed us Nikita Khrushchev's grave. It is fairly unobtrusive, yet there were many people around it. I asked her why he didn't have a bigger stone. She was surprised. "He was *just* a man," she said plainly. A few graves down from Khrushchev's was the tomb of the editor who published the first works of Solzhenitsyn.

We then drove out towards Moscow University. Irina told me that at the university students were granted up to eighty rubles — one hundred dollars — a month for their expenses. Laundry money. As we rode through the hills overlooking the Lenin Sports Complex and the city, we passed by the Russian National Ski-Jumping Team.

Last night's snow had melted away, but the jumpers were practicing on an eighty-meter run made out of polyethylene and a landing area made out of straw.

After a while we went back to the hotel, and the minute I walked into the lobby a dozen people asked me if I had heard anything new. "Anything new about what?" I said, looking dumbfounded. Well, it seems there is a strong possibility that we will not be playing the decisive game tomorrow night — or, for that matter, any other night. This afternoon Bobrov and Aleksander Gresko, the No. 2 official in the Soviet sports hierarchy, called Harry and Alan Eagleson and said that they had made no officiating agreement and that now they were going to select the two West Germans — Kompalla and Baader — to work in the eighth game. Harry and Al rushed over to the Palace of Sport and both sides met all afternoon without any success.

Harry and Al have told the Russians there will be no game if the West Germans referee. We made an agreement and kept our part of the bargain: Bergman was completely closemouthed last night. Early in the game, though, Boris Mikhailov skated past our bench a couple of times and yelled some Russian epithets at Ferguson. So we sent a note to their bench: "Bergman not saying anything to Bobrov, Mikhailov should shut up, too." Boris didn't come near our bench the rest of the night. Still, the Russians want to renege.

One problem with the negotiations, I understand, is that Andrei Starovoitov, the head of the Soviet Hockey Federation, is in Vienna at an International Hockey Federation meeting and the Russians have to clear everything with him. The conversations at the Palace of Sport pass through an interpreter to the Russians, then over the phone to Starovoitov in Vienna. Diplomacy. It's wonderful.

I saw Eagleson before dinner and he said that the Russians will have an answer at 6 P.M. Al thinks they will eventually stick to the agreement because of money reasons. They have sold the European television rights for a reported two hundred thousand dollars per game in advance, and the money for the eighth game already is in the bank. "They like dollars," Eagleson said. "I've found that a lot of times the Russians will let money make up their minds for them." At 6 P.M. Gary Smith, a Canadian attached to our embassy here, came in and huddled with Eagleson and Sinden to tell them the Russians said they would not have a decision until 11 P.M.

I tried to figure out what kind of psychology the Russians were using on us. For a while I thought they were trying to upset our composure and to destroy our concentration by causing uncertainty about whether or not the game would be played. Then I thought that maybe the brouhaha over the referees was a perfect out for me. If the game is not played, the series will end in a tie. I can rationalize that we are coming on and will win the game *and* the series. All of us, though, expect that the game will be played. Sometime, somehow, there will be a negotiated settlement, I'm sure. Still, the entire thing is upsetting.

To take my mind off hockey for a couple of hours, Lynda and I went to see *Anna Karenina,* a ballet based on the Tolstoi novel. We sat in the first row of a balcony box, about two tiers above the main level, so we had a perfect view as the prima ballerina of the Soviet Union, Maya Plisetskaya, put on a brilliant exhibition.

Back at the hotel we waited for news of the 11 P.M. decision. Again the Russians had no decision to announce. They wanted to sleep on it.

Pat Stapleton takes the puck from Yuri Blinov the hard way.

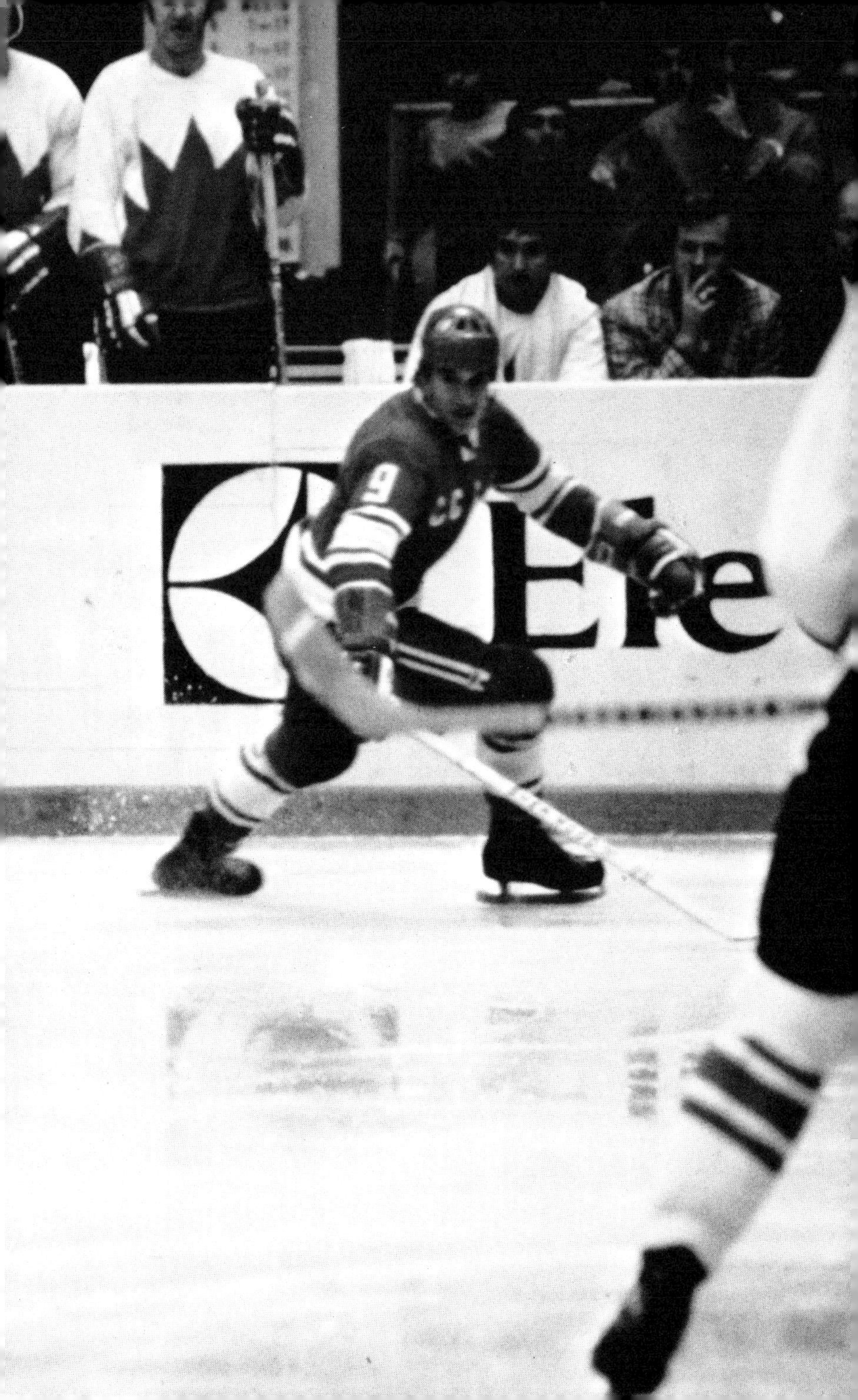

September 28

The Moscow Peace Talks are scheduled for the Palace of Sport at 10 A.M. At 9:35, Harry and Al dashed out of the Intourist and jumped into a car. At 9:37, Gresko jumped out of a car and dashed into the lobby of the Intourist. Nothing like a little mix-up to get the discussions under way. "They went thataway," someone told Gresko. So off he went after them.

We practiced while the negotiators were in session upstairs. I wondered what shape of table they were using for the talks. Was it round? Was it square? Was it rectangular? Who sat where? Was the interpreter a Russian or a Canadian? Was the connection to Starovoitov in Vienna clear? Was Gresko pounding his shoe on the table, like Khrushchev did that day at the U.N.? Very intriguing. Still, there was little doubt among the players that there would be a game. "Just be ready at 8 P.M., guys," was the tone of the workout.

Shortly after noontime, Sinden and Eagleson came back to the hotel and told us that a compromise had been worked out. Both teams agreed to pick one referee for the game. The Soviets selected one of the West Germans — Kompalla, who, ironically, wants to come to North America someday and officiate in the NHL. We picked Uve Dahlberg, the Swede, but he was bedded at his hotel with a bad case of the flu. So we had to choose between Franz Baader of West Germany and Rudy Batja of Czechoslovakia. We decided on Batja, who is an excellent official. "If Batja gets sick," Eagleson said, "we'll insist on a Russian referee rather than Baader."

Someone told me that Dahlberg's stomach problems

were the result of something he had eaten at breakfast. Suddenly I got a touch of paranoia about my breakfast food. Maybe I'll come down sick, too. I tried to sleep for an hour and a half but all I did was toss restlessly in bed. It was one of the most uncomfortable, tension-filled times of my life. For two days straight I had been extremely nervous. Even when I was doing something totally unrelated to hockey, the feeling was still there — the queasy stomach, rubber legs, fear. Later, as I walked down Gorki Street and into Red Square to get some fresh air, I tried to take deep breaths and relax my nerves.

Hey, the game has to be played. It will be played. Just make the best of it. Being nervous will hinder your performance. Forget about it. Please.

But talking to yourself makes for a very one-sided conversation. I tried to convince myself that it was just another big game. I had played for the NCAA Championship and I had played the seventh and final game for the Stanley Cup. What is there to worry about now? Unfortunately, I'm afraid that whoever listened didn't provide any help. My body simply refused to respond to what my mind was trying to rationalize. I was more nervous than ever.

I went upstairs to get a few things from the room and suddenly the phone rang. I picked it up but whoever was on the other end hung up. Then it rang again. It was Irina the interpreter-guide who drove us around Moscow a few days ago. She asked if Lynda was there, and I said no. Then she asked me if I could meet her in the lobby. I went down to see her, and she had a present for us: a very small handmade chess set. I was touched by the gesture, and I couldn't thank her enough.

Then we all went off to the rink. There were stacks and piles of new telegrams of goodwill on chairs and tables in the corridors of the dressing sections. Some classmates at McGill Law School sent one to me that I put in my locker. It read: "Super game on Sunday — don't forget Business Associations on Thursday." If I were back in Montreal right now, I'd probably be at the Business Associations lecture. But I'm here in Moscow, and The Game is only an hour away. Business Associations never sounded so good. What's Harry Sinden saying about the game? "It should be the greatest hockey game ever played." Well, I hope so.

In the room, and out on the ice during the warm-up, the guys were not as encouraging as they had been before the sixth game. Considering the pressure I felt myself, the absence of overt encouragement was a welcome relief. What had brought on their vocal expressions of encouragement the other night was their uncertainty about Ken Dryden. For this game, though, they felt it was not necessary, that I was back from the doldrums.

As we skated onto the ice the three thousand Canadian fans began to shout, "Da da Canada, nyet nyet Soviet." From the other end, though, the Russians responded with shrieking whistles and chants of *shaibu, shaibu, shaibu*. They introduced the players and played both national anthems, then we exchanged gifts at center ice. For this game we gave the Russian players three-gallon hats, and Kharlamov — back in the lineup after recovering from his injury — immediately put his hat on his head and skated towards the bench. Game time.

I always like to handle the puck a couple of times right at the start of the game, and the Russians obliged by taking two good shots within the first minute. I stopped both of them without any difficulty — and then the nervousness, the tension seemed to leave. But soon we ran into some trouble of our own making. Batja called a tripping penalty on Bill White at 2:25 of the first period, and just thirty-six seconds later Kompalla sent Peter Mahovlich to the box for holding. Why? Why? Let's settle down, guys. We are going to get ourselves in deep trouble.

The Russians organized their power play beautifully and passed the puck around precisely in our zone. Someone shot. I kicked it out with my left pad, but the rebound slid across to Yakushev — why didn't *he* get the flu? — and he fired it under my arm. *Boom!* The Russians led 1–0. A minute or so later we saw another example of the "spirit of understanding." J. P. Parise was checking one of the Russian forwards near our net, working him over pretty aggressively. Kompalla, the referee closest to the play, waved the play safe — meaning no penalty. However, Batja, who was at least fifty feet away from Parise, raised his right arm and pointed at Parise, signaling for a penalty. As in Sweden, when Kompalla called a penalty after his partner, Franz Baader, had whistled it safe, this was a contradictory judgment and another indictment of the two-referee system. You would think that for their own sake referees would never give a safe sign.

Needless to say, when Batja finally blew his whistle to stop play after we gained control of the puck, Parise exploded — and so did the other Canadian players on the ice and everyone on the bench. J. P. bolted towards the referees and began to berate them vehemently. So Batja tacked on a ten-minute misconduct penalty, too. Now J. P. was really steaming, and he impulsively brought up his stick and started to bring it down against the boards between Batja and Kompalla. Fortunately, he stopped halfway, but it was enough to scare everyone, including J. P. Shaken by the scene, Batja immediately added a game misconduct.

On the bench we lost our composure. Someone even

threw a chair onto the ice. All hell broke loose. Towels, sticks, gloves, pucks all came flying over the boards and onto the ice. The Canadian fans in the stands began to chant, "Let's go home, let's go home." Eagleson leaped out of his seat across the ice, hurdled the railing, landed upright, and then ran around the boards to our bench. Right then our fans began to litter the ice with rolls of toilet paper. Meanwhile, a few dozen Russian militiamen marched in close-order rank to our penalty box and surrounded it three deep. And behind our bench, Eagleson and Gresko, who had not spoken a friendly word to one another for a few days, were waving fingers at each other. It was a very chaotic scene, to say the least.

All this time, the Russian players sat on their bench or on top of the boards, looking bored. As I watched things myself, I had a few frightening thoughts. We still have fifty-six minutes to play and we're already down a goal. Calm down. Let's regain our composure. I could imagine the Russians scoring a quick goal or two while we were still hot over Parise's penalty and banishment. So I skated to our bench and tried to help calm everyone down. Fortunately for us, I think, it took the attendants almost fifteen minutes to clean up the ice, and during that time our guys seemed to cool down. In fact, when the game finally resumed after a total delay of almost twenty-seven minutes, we were completely composed.

Two and a half minutes later, we got a break. Batja detected Gennady Tsygankov interfering with someone in front of the Russians' goal, and off he went for two minutes. Just seventeen seconds later Phil Esposito tied the score as he rapped in a loose puck at the goal mouth.

Strange. For seven games the referees had practically ignored what Canadians think is interference, and now they suddenly were calling interference penalties. At

9:27 of the first period, Ron Ellis, who was assigned to follow Kharlamov all over the ice after the game in Winnipeg and who has shut him off the scoreboard ever since, went out for interfering with him. Nineteen seconds later Vladimir Petrov got an interference penalty, too. At 12:51, Batja sent Cournoyer to the penalty box for interfering with Aleksander Maltsev. Five interference penalties in less than thirteen minutes.

While Cournoyer was in the box, Lutchenko put the Russians ahead 2–1 with a long screen shot that I never saw until it was past me. We continued to press, and with just about three minutes left in the period Brad Park — playing his best game of the series by far — stole the puck at center ice and fed it to Jean Ratelle. Working the give-and-go perfectly, the two Rangers bore down on the right wing. Ratelle delayed just long enough to lure the defenseman out, then fed the puck ahead to Park. Brad put a great move on Tretiak as he cut in off the right side and flipped the puck past the goalie's right shoulder. A classic goal. So the score was tied again.

I have mentioned the netting that the Russians have installed in place of glass behind the net. In the opening seconds of the second period, Yakushev fired a hard shot at me from about forty-five feet out. The shot obviously was going to be wide of the net, so I had two choices: I could go out, catch the puck, and drop it for one of our defensemen; or I could let the shot go, watch the puck rebound off the netting, and play it accordingly. The danger involved in the first choice is that it is basically a gamble. Oftentimes you have to move a great distance to get at the puck, increasing the possibility of it bouncing off your glove and caroming towards the goal. All in all, I felt that trying to catch the puck was not really worth it in this situation. So I let the shot go.

The puck snapped into the netting and came off like it had been shot from a sling — right at the back of my head. In fact, if I had not moved my head at the last second, the puck would have hit it and bounced down into the goal. Instead, it boomeranged out to about twenty-five feet in front and landed right in the middle of Vladimir Shadrin's stick. Bingo! Suddenly we were down 3–2. I was really upset.

The worst thing about the mesh netting is that it is so inconsistent. Tony, E. J. and I spent a long time studying the results of shots fired into the netting during practice and came away without any definite conclusions. If a puck hits a taut area near the support posts, then it shoots back out with the boomerang effect. But there are so many variables of speed, height, rotation, and force in every shot that it is impossible to predict accurately what will happen every time. I should have caught the damn puck.

So, we were down again, 3–2, but still we didn't quit. Right after the ten-minute mark of the period we tied the score at 3–3, thanks to a great play by Rod "Mad Dog" Gilbert. For the longest time — at least five or six seconds — Rod stickhandled the puck near the boards, about halfway between the goal line and the blue line to the right of Tretiak. I don't know why but the Russians did not bother to check him. While Rod was stickhandling, Bill White — the right defenseman at the other side of the ice — sneaked down the right wing and as he got to the goal mouth Gilbert fired a perfect pass across the ice. Tretiak never had a chance as White calmly tipped the puck into the net.

Normally in situations like this, much of the emotion of the game depends upon the ability of goaltenders to make what the players call "big" saves. I made the first one, stopping Boris Mikhailov on a two-on-one break at the crease. It gave me a great lift, and I hoped that it would give the other guys a great lift, too. But on the ensuing face-off the Russians scored again. Phil Esposito beat Petrov to the draw, so much so that his wingers busted for the other end of the ice, leaving their wings uncovered. But the puck bounced crazily and landed on Shadrin's stick. In a flash that man Yakushev got the puck in front and shot it into the corner. Now it was 4–3, and a few minutes later it was 5–3 as they scored their third power-play goal of the game. Once again, Yakushev set it up. For almost twenty seconds he skated around and around with the puck inside our blue line, all the while waiting for his teammates to get themselves in position. Then he passed the puck across the ice to defenseman Vasily Vasiliev. After holding it for a few seconds, Vasiliev moved in from the boards to my left and fired into a maze of players just outside the crease. hoping for a deflection. Unfortunately, he got it as the puck tipped off one of our defenseman's knees and caromed into the corner. T-R-O-U-B-L-E. We had to score at least three goals to win.

A minute later the Russians almost scored again on a three-on-one break but Shadrin fired the puck into my pads as I slid across the goal mouth. That same play would have been an easy goal in Montreal four weeks ago. They played the three-on-one perfectly. The lead man dropped it over to the right wing who, in turn, slipped it across the crease to Shadrin. In the opening game of the series, before I changed my style and became a stay-in-the-net goalie, I would have gone out after either the first man or the second and left the third man to chance. Now I was still in my net, and when the pass went to Shadrin I instinctively slid across to block the shot. It was probably the best save I made in the entire series.

A few seconds later Phil Esposito made probably a better save, though. Yuri Blinov had the puck and was cutting across the net. I moved with him, and as I did he shoveled the puck behind me towards the vacated net. But there was Esposito, coming from nowhere, to intercept the puck about a foot short of the goal line and skate it out of trouble. Goaltending runs in the Esposito family. Whew!

Despite everything, we were not totally dejected in the dressing room. As Tony Esposito said, "Hey, if they can get five goals on me in one period, we can get three goals on Tretiak in one period." We had to score an early goal in order to build up some momentum, though, and avoid having to play an all-out offensive game, leaving defense to chance — usually a disastrous strategy. Phil got it for us. Peter Mahovlich, taking Parise's place at left wing, skated around the net and flipped a hard pass out to Phil, who was in his customary position in the slot, about ten feet in front of Tretiak. Phil gloved the puck like a first baseman and dropped it onto the ice, right onto his stick. Tretiak never had a chance — and we were back in the game. It was our game now, and for the rest of the period I was practically a spectator as we peppered Tretiak with hard shots from all over the ice. We almost tied the score at the ten-minute mark of the period but Jean Ratelle's backhander flew just over the open net. Still, we were pressing well — and the Russians didn't seem capable of stopping us now.

At 12:56 Yvan Cournoyer tied the score — or did he? Park kept the puck in at the blue line and shot it in front of Tretiak. Espo took a whack at it, and for a time it seemed as though all ten players up the ice were flailing away at the puck. But Cournoyer got it and rifled it past Tretiak. I saw it myself from almost two hundred feet down the ice. But the red light never went on. It was in the net, though. We knew it. The Russians knew it. And, most important, the referees knew it.

All of a sudden there was a big commotion over near the penalty box, across the ice from the player benches. Obviously irate at the goal judge for not turning on the light, Eagleson had hopped over the railing onto the floor again and was trying to barge through a couple of dozen militiamen. "I wanted to go down and punch the damn goal judge," Eagleson said. "Here we had tied the most important hockey game ever played and our three thousand fans here and the twenty million people watching on television in Canada did not know what had happened." The militiamen surrounded Eagleson and began to hustle him out of the rink, carrying him by his elbows and lifting his feet off the ground.

Peter Mahovlich was the first Canadian player to notice the commotion. "All I saw was the Bird [Eagleson] and all those cops around him," Peter said. He charged across the ice, waving his stick, and right behind him were eighteen other hockey players, Sinden, Ferguson, the trainers and a couple of guys who weren't playing in the game. Some of our guys hopped over the boards and rescued Eagleson from the militiamen. And then, with Al in their midst, our guys went back across the ice to the bench.

It was a comic situation. Here we were springing someone from a national militia and taking him to an unassailable position at our team bench.

Suddenly I had that feeling again. My muscles were tight. The next goal no doubt would be decisive. Externally, internally — there was terrible pressure. I remember only one thing about the last seven minutes of the game: Paul Henderson scored with just thirty-four seconds to play. I can still see us moving into their end

Paul Henderson celebrates winning the series for Canada by his goal in the last thirty-four seconds of the eighth game. (He also scored winning goals in the sixth and seventh games!).

and noticing on the clock that there was less than a minute to play. Then the puck went against the boards, and Esposito and Cournoyer were battling for it. Henderson, meanwhile, was standing near Tretiak, scorned by the other Russians. And then the puck came out of the corner and right in front of Henderson. Paul shot. I saw it go in. I saw it go in. Again there was no light. But again, there was no question that the puck went in.

Henderson was jumping up and down, and then suddenly all hell broke loose as we all streamed down the ice to salute him. Geez Murphy, what a guy to have on your side in the clutch! He had scored the winning goal in the sixth game. He had scored the winning goal in the last minutes of the seventh game. And now he had scored the go-ahead goal with just thirty-four seconds to play in the deciding game of the World Series. I can't remember the last time I left my goal to skate to the opposite end of the ice and congratulate someone, but I set a record for the one-hundred-eighty-foot padded skate and joined the mob around Henderson.

Then I realized there were still thirty-four seconds to play. The Russians had scored twice in nine seconds the other night. It was, without doubt, the longest thirty-four seconds I have ever played. It seemed like thirty-four days, but after everything we had been through, we weren't going to let anything crush us now. We checked furiously and they never got off a decent shot. It was over. 6–5. The Canadians were singing "Oh Canada" in the stands and waving their miniature Canadian flags. And then they started that incessant cheer: "We're No. 1, We're No. 1."

We are.

In the dressing room the players, the wives and the officials broke out in a spontaneous "Oh Canada." It is easy to become an instant patriot by singing the national anthem before a game, but this was totally sincere. I'm not particularly patriotic or nationalistic, and I'm not a flag-waver — but singing the national anthem in that dressing room seemed like the only thing to do.

I talked with Eagleson briefly, and he told me that Henderson's goal prevented another major crisis. After the second period, Gresko had stopped Eagleson in the corridor to the locker rooms and told him that if the game ended in a tie the Russians would declare themselves the winner of the series on the basis of total goals scored. "Like hell you will," Eagleson screamed back at Gresko, and for once the Russian did not need his interpreter to understand exactly what Al meant. As it turned out, the Russians did outscore us: thirty-two to thirty-one over the eight games.

After the initial outburst in the room, the guys suddenly became very quiet. We were exhausted emotionally. Exhausted physically. Totally spent. I just looked around the room: everyone's uniform was soaked with sweat. I felt really proud . . . for all of us. I didn't know more than a handful of them six weeks ago, but now I felt that I knew every one of them in a way you rarely know anyone. We had gone from the heights to the depths — and now we were back on top again.

We drove back to the hotel for steak and a night of celebration. A team celebration. As the series progressed, it was plain to see that we had become a team, that we were no longer thirty-five separate guys. You become a team, I think, by having to go through bad times. By overcoming adversity. We had done that. Right now we were genuinely and deeply happy for one another. In a week, most of us will be on different teams again and will be trying to defeat one another once again. Maybe even with more desire than before, because that's how friends are. But we shared something important and that is a great and lasting feeling.

It was bloody over. There was nothing more to say, but we did walk down to the Metropole Hotel and stay for a few minutes at a reception the Russians had scheduled for both teams. Six or eight Soviet players were there, and I really wanted to say something to them. Where was Irina? Who could help me communicate with these men? The sad thing about this entire series is that we never got to know the Russian players as people.

But we certainly learned who the individual players were. I'll bet that before the first game in Montreal the average player on Team Canada knew the names of only three or four people attached to the Russian team. Tarasov, the old coach; Anatoli Firsov, who never played in the series because of the combination of a knee injury and creeping old age; and maybe Aleksander Ragulin, the defenseman who has been around for almost a decade. Now, at the end, Yakushev, Maltsev, Kharlamov, Lutchenko and Tretiak are big names to us. They are like Mahovlich, Orr, Esposito, Ratelle and Hull. And we also know of Vasiliev and Tsygankov. As we left, we sort of said good-bye with hand signals. Thumbs up.

Over in a corner, just as we were leaving, Eagleson was communicating with Gresko and some other Russian officials about the goal-light incidents. Apparently Al went down to the goal judge's seat long after the crowd had left the Palace of Sport and flicked the switch that turns on the light. He flicked it eight times in all — and each time the red light went on. The Russians were extremely embarrassed about the incident, and now they were apologizing to Eagleson for what had happened.

As far as I'm concerned, the Soviets are a great hockey team, and I have great respect for them. We were extremely fortunate to win this series, believe me. But as the night wore on and the champagne took effect, many fans began to think differently. I couldn't believe it.

"If we played them in mid-season with some games under our belts, we'd probably beat them eight straight."

"They couldn't maintain the pace in the NHL for seventy-eight games and then the Stanley Cup play-offs."

Here I was still thinking about how difficult the series had been, about how much harder players had worked in this series than they ever had worked before, and how lucky we were to come out of the series with a 4–3–1 edge, thanks to a goal with only thirty-four seconds to play. And here we were putting them down. Even though we won the last three games and the series, they were all one-goal victories. And now we were talking about our great superiority. To me, it was a sad moment in a great series. These feelings of superiority did not fit the occasion. And I, for one, don't believe that we are that superior.

September 29

Last night I didn't sleep at all. The celebration lasted until dawn, as thousands of Canadians milled around the Intourist dollar bars and bought champagne and more champagne for everyone in sight. Around 5 A.M. I opened a window to get some air and heard some happy Canadians — obviously inebriated — singing "Oh Canada," and then I looked out and saw them parading in the direction of Red Square. These people will never forget this trip, I'm sure. Many of them had to beg and borrow to pay for it, and I know some people who will be paying off on their charge cards for the next three years. In ten years, when people are still talking about Henderson's goal, I imagine that there will be a couple of hundred thousand people around Canada who'll be saying, "Yes, we were there." But the great thing is that the people who were actually there will never regret that they were present.

At 6 A.M., I had to start packing for the trip to Prague. We are playing the Czechoslovakian Nationals there tomorrow night.

It started to snow as we drove to the airport. Normally, players never dwell on games the next day, but I'll bet the word "unbelievable" was used in every sentence of conversation during the long ride from Moscow. The Russians cleared us through customs in record time again, and Ambassador Robert Ford was there to congratulate us and read a telegram from Prime Minister Trudeau.

Vsevolod Bobrov, the Russian coach, also checked in for the Aeroflot flight to Prague. "I'm going down to scout the Canadians again," he said.

Prague is a beautiful city. At the airport I met a kid named Ludek whom I had met three years ago in Prague when I came here with the Canadian National Team. He is an unbelievable Canadian hockey fan. One of his prize possessions is a Montreal Canadiens sweater that his mother knitted for him. He wore it all the time three years ago, and he wore it again today at the airport. He had pictures and books for all the Canadian players to autograph. One of his friends is probably the only kid in Europe — or even North America — who wears a Portland Buckaroos jacket. He is, he said, the only member of the Buckaroos fan club that lives outside

Oregon. I also met an old friendly enemy from my Ivy League days, a former Yale hockey player named John Cole who is playing hockey in Switzerland now.

September 30

I don't want to take anything away from the Czechs, but we are all really regretting that we have to play this game tonight. Although the Czechs are the world champions, they really are not as good as the Russians. So we could be deeply embarrassed if we lose. We have nothing to gain. Mentally we're certainly not ready for them because we peaked in the eighth game against the Russians less than forty-eight hours ago, and now the natural letdown has set in.

Before the game Frank Mahovlich cracked us up with his instructions on defense for the players. "Gentlemen," he intoned, "please watch your Czechs."

It was a happy, singing crowd, unlike the placid one in Moscow, and when the players were introduced individually, the fourteen thousand people in the arena cheered noisily. The biggest reception, though, was for Stan Mikita, who was born in Czechoslovakia and didn't leave the country until he was seven years old. Stan's mother, in fact, still lives here with all of his brothers and sisters, and they were all at the game. The fans gave Stan a standing ovation for about three minutes, and Stan, in turn, acknowledged the greeting by waving in all directions. It was a touching tribute, and Stan was deeply moved.

I played the whole game in goal. We took a 2–0 lead in the first period, but then we fell apart as the Czechs roared back to take a 3–2 lead. But we pulled another one out of the hat — this time with only four seconds to play. Jean-Paul Parise got credit for a goal that Serge Savard scored from the crease after Harry had removed me for an extra skater.

Just think, now, of all the embarrassment we saved ourselves by tying the second game of the Sweden series with a shorthanded goal in the last minute; by beating the Russians three times by one goal and ultimately beating them with just thirty-four seconds left in the series; and by tying the Czechs at 19:56 of the third period.

Back to Canada.

October 1

As our chartered jet flew from Prague to London and then on to Montreal and finally Toronto, I had a chance to relax with my thoughts and some old Canadian newspapers. According to the printed reports, there is a real debate raging in Canada over the behavior of the Team Canada players in Moscow. A number of writers suggested that we disgraced our country. In the letters-to-the-editor columns, notable people wrote to complain about our deportment overseas. Dr. Penfield, a famous neurosurgeon, said that he will feel embarrassed the next time he attends a conference of neurosurgeons in Moscow. They did not like our choke signs and our so-called dirty gestures.

Well, as far as I am concerned, many of our reactions were quite understandable; in fact, I don't believe we reacted any differently than we would have in an NHL game. We were told to play our game — and we did. The Russians, of course, did not play like an NHL team, thereby offering a sharp contrast. If you are a critic of the NHL style, then you have a right to criticize us. If not, then you are taking a cheap second guess at something you've never questioned before. One reason for our deportment at times was the problem of language. You cannot tell a Russian or a Swede that you'll get him later after what you think is a dirty play, so you must resort to sign language.

And these people said that Team Canada hurt the country diplomatically. Well, I'm not certain that the Soviet opinion of Canadians has changed. After all, Canadian amateur teams acted the same way when they were overseas. Besides, what does "hurt diplomatically" really mean? Did we hurt the trade balances? I doubt it.

What really irritates me, though, is the great, great criticism that Eagleson is getting. I did not know him very well before the series, and I had reservations about him. When you don't know him, it's easy to dislike him. All you ever see of Eagleson are his quotes and interviews, and he usually comes across pretty strong in print. All I can say is that he had the toughest job imaginable for six weeks — except, of course, for the job that Tretiak and I had in the eighth game. I don't think anyone wanted to switch with either of us at that time. But Eagleson did his job perfectly.

Not only did Eagleson have to satisfy thirty-five players and all the Russian hockey officials, but he was the housemother for the three thousand Canadian fans. Anything wrong? See Al. "Al, my sheets are dirty." "Al, my room's too small." "My steak came too rare today, Al." "My borscht was greasy, Al." "Where's Eagleson?" "Eaglebird, what can you do about getting me ten more tickets for tonight's game?"

Russians are not that difficult to deal with once you get past the initial answers of "impossible" and "can't do it" and "never." Fortunately for all of us, Eagleson knew that the only way to handle the Russians was to call their bluff. Like, "Okay, *you* can't do that, then we can't do this." For instance, on the day we were scheduled to take a tour of the Kremlin, the Russians insisted that the husbands travel in one bus and the wives in another. Eagleson simply told the Russians, "The wives and husbands go together." They said, "Impossible." "Okay," Eagleson said, "none of us will go." Suddenly it was not so impossible anymore. Another time, the Russians provided circus tickets for the players but forgot about the wives. "No wives, no players," Eagleson told the Russians, and almost instantly the wives were given tickets.

I don't know of anyone else who could have led us through this series as well as Eagleson. Sure, maybe some of his public actions were questionable, but it is unfortunate that the public never got a glimpse of what he did behind the scenes.

And a few other thoughts: 1) playing the series in September was ridiculous; 2) spending eight days in Sweden was ridiculous; 3) playing without all our best players — like Bobby Hull, for instance — was ridiculous.

I think we have all grown up these past six weeks. From an unswerving commitment to the belief that Canadians are unquestionably the best in the world and that our style is right because we invented the game and developed it, the feeling now seems to have changed to an awareness that the Russians have something going, too. Now there seems to be an appreciation for discipline and passing and skating, and at the same time, there is a questioning of the old NHL standards of conditioning and preparedness. Both the Russians and the Canadians have an amazing amount to learn.

It's over now. We'll be landing in Montreal in a few minutes. J. P. Parise and Bill Goldsworthy of the Minnesota North Stars have been bugging me for the last hour or so, mimicking the voice of the public-address announcer in the Montreal Forum. "North Stars goal scored by Number 8, Bill Goldsworthy. Assist to Number 11, Jean-Paul Parise." And "North Stars goal scored by Number 11, Jean-Paul Parise. Assist to Number 8, Bill Goldsworthy."

"When?" I say to them. "1975?"

"No," J. P. says. "Next Saturday night, October 7, in the Forum. See you then."

OFFICIAL SUMMARIES AND STATISTICS F TEAM CANADA'S INTERNATIONAL TOUR
September, 1972

Prepared by Ron Andrews,
Director of Information and Statistician,
National Hockey League

TEAM CANADA VS. SOVIET UNION

Game #1, September 2, at Montreal.
Soviet Union 7, Team Canada 3

PLAYERS ON ICE

Soviet Union: Gusev, Lutchenko, Kuzkin, Ragulin, Vasiliev, Tsygankov, Blinov, Maltsev, Zimin, Mishakov, Mikhailov, Yakushev, Petrov, Kharlamov, Vikulov, Shadrin, Liapkin, Paladiev.

Team Canada: Bergman, Park, Ellis, P. Esposito, Gilbert, Hadfield, Cournoyer, Berenson, Seiling, Ratelle, Henderson, P. Mahovlich, Redmond, Lapointe, Awrey, F. Mahovlich, Clarke.

GOALTENDERS

Soviet Union: Tretiak, 60 minutes, 3 goals against.
Team Canada: Dryden, 60 minutes, 7 goals against.

SUMMARY

First Period

1. Team Canada: P. Esposito (F. Mahovlich, Bergman) 00.30
2. Team Canada: Henderson (Clarke) 6:32
3. Soviet Union: Zimin (Yakushev, Shadrin) 11:40
4. Soviet Union: Petrov (Mikhailov) 17:28. Shorthanded goal

PENALTIES: Henderson (tripping) 1:03, Yakushev (tripping) 7:04, Mikhailov (tripping) 15:11, Ragulin (tripping) 17:19

Second Period

5. Soviet Union: Kharlamov (Maltsev) 2:40
6. Soviet Union: Kharlamov (Maltsev) 10:18

PENALTIES: Clarke (slashing) 5:16, Lapointe (slashing) 12:53

Third Period

7. Team Canada: Clarke (Ellis, Henderson) 8:22
8. Soviet Union: Mikhailov (Blinov) 13:32
9. Soviet Union: Zimin 14:29
10. Soviet Union: Yakushev (Shadrin) 18:37

PENALTIES: Kharlamov (high-sticking) 14:45, Lapointe (cross-checking) 19:41

SHOTS ON GOAL BY					SHOTS AT GOAL BY				
Soviet					Soviet				
Union	10	10	10 —	30	Union	27	24	21 —	72
Team					Team				
Canada	10	10	12 —	32	Canada	22	19	20 —	61

Game #2, September 4, at Toronto.
Team Canada 4, Soviet Union 1

PLAYERS ON ICE

Soviet Union: Gusev, Lutchenko, Kuzkin, Ragulin, Tsygan-
kov, Starshinov, Maltsev, Zimin, Mishakov, Mikhailov,
Yakushev, Petrov, Kharlamov, Shadrin, Anisin, Liapkin,
Paladiev.
Team Canada: Bergman, Stapleton, Park, Ellis, P. Esposito,
Goldsworthy, Cournoyer, Cashman, White, Henderson,
P. Mahovlich, Mikita, Parise, Savard, Lapointe, F. Ma-
hovlich, Clarke.

GOALTENDERS

Soviet Union: Tretiak, 60 minutes, 4 goals against.
Team Canada: T. Esposito, 60 minutes, 1 goal against.

SUMMARY

First Period
No Scoring
PENALTIES: Park (cross-checking) 10:08, Henderson (trip-
ping) 15:19

Second Period
1. Team Canada: P. Esposito (Park, Cashman) 7:14
PENALTIES: Gusev (tripping) 2:07, Soviet Union bench
minor (served by Zimin) 4:13, Bergman (tripping)
15:16, Tsygankov (slashing) 19:54, Kharlamov (10-
minute misconduct) 19:54

Third Period
2. Team Canada: Cournoyer (Park) 1:19. Power-Play goal
3. Soviet Union: Yakushev (Liapkin, Zimin) 5:53. Power-
play goal
4. Team Canada: P. Mahovlich (P. Esposito) 6:47. Shorthanded goal
5. Team Canada: F. Mahovlich (Mikita, Cournoyer) 8:59
PENALTIES: Clark (slashing) 5:13, Stapleton (hooking)
6:14

[191]

SHOTS ON GOAL BY				SHOTS AT GOAL BY			
Soviet Union	7	5	9 — 21	Soviet Union	23	9	16 — 48
Team Canada	10	16	10 — 36	Team Canada	15	26	19 — 60

Game #3, September 6, at Winnipeg.
Soviet Union 4, Team Canada 4

PLAYERS ON ICE

Soviet Union: Gusev, Lutchenko, Kuzkin, Vasiliev, Tsygan-
kov, Maltsev, Mishakov, Mikhailov, Shatalov, Yakushev,
Petrov, Kharlamov, Shadrin, Solodukhin, Anisin, Lebedev,
Bodunov.
Team Canada: Bergman, Stapleton, Park, Ellis, P. Esposito,
Cournoyer, Cashman, White, Ratelle, Henderson, P.
Mahovlich, Mikita, Parise, Savard, Lapointe, F. Mahov-
lich, Clarke.

GOALTENDERS

Soviet Union: Tretiak, 60 minutes, 4 goals against.
Team Canada: T. Esposito, 60 minutes, 4 goals against.

SUMMARY

First Period
1. Team Canada: Parise (White, P. Esposito) 1:54
2. Soviet Union: Petrov 3:15. Shorthanded goal
3. Team Canada: Ratelle (Cournoyer, Bergman) 18:25
PENALTIES: Vasiliev (elbowing) 3:02, Cashman (slashing)
   8:01, Parise (interference) 15:47

Second Period
4. Team Canada: P. Esposito (Cashman, Parise) 4:19
5. Soviet Union: Kharlamov (Tsygankov) 12:56. Shorthanded goal
6. Team Canada: Henderson (Clarke, Ellis) 13:47
7. Soviet Union: Lebedev (Vasiliev, Anisin) 14:59
8. Soviet Union: Bodunov (Anisin) 18:28
PENALTIES: Petrov (interference) 4:46, Lebedev (tripping)
   11:00

Third Period
No Scoring
PENALTIES: White (slashing), Mishakov (slashing) 1:33,
   Cashman (minor, slashing, and 10-minute misconduct)
   10:44

SHOTS ON GOAL BY				SHOTS AT GOAL BY			
Soviet Union	9	8	8 — 25	Soviet Union	23	21	25 — 69
Team Canada	15	17	6 — 38	Team Canada	23	30	14 — 67

Game #4, September 8, at Vancouver.
Soviet Union 5, Team Canada 3

Soviet Union: Lutchenko, Kuzkin, Ragulin, Vasiliev, Tsy-
gankov, Blinov, Maltsev, Mikhailov, Yakushev, Petrov,
Kharlamov, Vikulov, Shadrin, Anisin, Lebedev, Bodunov,
Paladiev.

Team Canada: Bergman, Stapleton, Park, Ellis, P. Esposito,
Gilbert, Goldsworthy, D. Hull, Hadfield, Cournoyer, Seil-
ing, White, Henderson, Awrey, F. Mahovlich, Clarke,
Perreault.

GOALTENDERS

Soviet Union: Tretiak, 60 minutes, 3 goals against.
Team Canada: Dryden, 60 minutes, 5 goals against.

SUMMARY

First Period
1. Soviet Union: Mikhailov (Lutchenko, Petrov) 2:01.
   Power-play goal
2. Soviet Union: Mikhailov (Lutchenko, Petrov) 7:29.
   Power-play goal
PENALTIES: Goldsworthy (cross-checking) 1:24, Goldsworthy (elbowing) 5:58, P. Esposito (tripping) 19:29

Second Period
3. Team Canada: Perreault 5:37
4. Soviet Union: Blinov (Petrov, Mikhailov) 6:34
5. Soviet Union: Vikulov (Kharlamov, Maltsev) 13:52
PENALTY: Kuzkin (tripping) 8:39

Third Period
6. Team Canada: Goldsworthy (P. Esposito, Bergman)
   6:54
7. Soviet Union: Shadrin (Yakushev, Vasiliev) 11:05
8. Team Canada: D. Hull (P. Esposito, Goldsworthy)
   19:38
PENALTY: Petrov (holding) 2:01

[194]

SHOTS ON GOAL BY				
Soviet Union	11	14	6	— 31
Team Canada	10	8	23	— 41

SHOTS AT GOAL BY				
Soviet Union	23	30	15	— 68
Team Canada	23	17	27	— 67

PLAYERS ON ICE

Team Canada: Bergman, Stapleton, Park, Ellis, P. Esposito, Gilbert, Cournoyer, Seiling, White, Ratelle, Henderson, P. Mahovlich, Parise, Lapointe, F. Mahovlich, Clarke, Perreault.

Soviet Union: Gusev, Lutchenko, Kuzkin, Ragulin, Tsygankov, Blinov, Maltsev, Mishakov, Mikhailov, Yakushev, Petrov, Kharlamov, Vikulov, Shadrin, Anisin, Liapkin, Martyniuk.

GOALTENDERS

Team Canada: T. Esposito, 60 minutes, 5 goals against.
Soviet Union: Tretiak, 60 minutes, 4 goals against.

SUMMARY

First Period
1. Team Canada: Parise (Perreault, Gilbert) 15:30
PENALTIES: Ellis (tripping) 3:49, Kharlamov (slashing) 12:25

Second Period
2. Team Canada: Clarke (Henderson) 2:36
3. Team Canada: Henderson (Lapointe, Clarke) 11:58
PENALTIES: Ellis (slashing) 5:38, Kharlamov (holding) 5:38, Bergman (roughing) 8:13, White (slashing) 20:00, Blinov (slashing) 20:00

Third Period
4. Soviet Union: Blinov (Petrov, Kuzkin) 3:34
5. Team Canada: Henderson (Clarke) 4:56
6. Soviet Union: Anisin (Liapkin, Yakushev) 9:05
7. Soviet Union: Shadrin (Anisin) 9:13
8. Soviet Union: Gusev (Ragulin, Kharlamov) 11:41
9. Soviet Union: Vikulov (Kharlamov) 14:46
PENALTIES: Clarke (holding) 10:25, Tsygankov (high-sticking) 10:25, Yakushev (hooking) 15:48

SHOTS ON GOAL BY				SHOTS AT GOAL BY			
Team				Team			
Canada	12	13	12 — 37	Canada	18	23	20 — 61
Soviet				Soviet			
Union	9	13	11 — 33	Union	26	24	25 — 75

Game #6, September 24, at Moscow.
Team Canada 3, Soviet Union 2

PLAYERS ON ICE

Team Canada: Bergman, Stapleton, Park, Ellis, P. Esposito, Gilbert, D. Hull, Cournoyer, Berenson, White, Ratelle, Henderson, P. Mahovlich, Parise, Savard, Lapointe, Clarke.

Soviet Union: Lutchenko, Ragulin, Vasiliev, Tsygankov, Maltsev, Mikhailov, Shatalov, Yakushev, Petrov, Kharlamov, Vikulov, Shadrin, Anisin, Lebedev, Bodunov, Liapkin, Volchkov.

GOALTENDERS

Team Canada: Dryden, 60 minutes, 2 goals against.
Soviet Union: Tretiak, 60 minutes, 3 goals against.

SUMMARY

First Period
No Scoring
PENALTIES: Bergman (tripping) 10:21, P. Esposito (double minor, charging) 13:11

Second Period
1. Soviet Union: Liapkin (Yakushev, Shadrin) 1:12
2. Team Canada: D. Hull (Gilbert) 5:13
3. Team Canada: Cournoyer (Berenson) 6:21
4. Team Canada: Henderson 6:36
5. Soviet Union: Yakushev (Shadrin, Liapkin) 17:11. Power-play goal
PENALTIES: Ragulin (interference) 2:09, Lapointe (roughing) 8:29, Vasiliev (roughing) 8:29, Clarke (minor, slashing, and 10-minute misconduct) 10:12, D. Hull (slashing) 17.02, P. Esposito (major, high-sticking) 17:46, Team Canada bench minor (served by Cournoyer) 17:46

Third Period
No Scoring
PENALTY: Ellis (holding) 17:39

SHOTS ON GOAL BY				SHOTS AT GOAL BY			
Team				Team			
Canada	7	8	7 — 22	Canada	18	10	17 — 45
Soviet				Soviet			
Union	12	8	9 — 29	Union	23	19	15 — 57

Game #7, September 26, at Moscow.
Team Canada 4, Soviet Union 3

PLAYERS ON ICE

Team Canada: Bergman, Stapleton, Park, Ellis, P. Esposito, Gilbert, Goldsworthy, D. Hull, Cournoyer, White, Ratelle, Henderson, P. Mahovlich, Parise, Savard, Lapointe, Clarke.

Soviet Union: Gusev, Lutchenko, Kuzkin, Ragulin, Vasiliev, Tsygankov, Blinov, Maltsev, Mishakov, Mikhailov, Yakushev, Petrov, Vikulov, Shadrin, Anisin, Liapkin, Volchkov.

GOALTENDERS

Team Canada: T. Esposito, 60 minutes, 3 goals against.
Soviet Union: Tretiak, 60 minutes, 4 goals against.

SUMMARY

First Period
1. Team Canada: P. Esposito (Ellis, Henderson) 4:09
2. Soviet Union: Yakushev (Shadrin, Liapkin) 10:17
3. Soviet Union: Petrov (Vikulov, Tsygankov) 16:27. Power-play goal
4. Team Canada: P. Esposito (Savard, Parise) 17:34
PENALTIES: Mikhailov (tripping) 2:00, P. Mahovlich (roughing) 5:16, Mishakov (holding) 5:16, Mishakov (holding) 11:09, P. Esposito (cross-checking) 12:39, White (interference) 15:45

Second Period
No Scoring
PENALTIES: Gilbert (hooking) 00:59, Parise (slashing) 6:04, Anisin (hooking) 6:11, P. Esposito (roughing) 12:44, Kuzkin (roughing) 12:44, Parise (roughing) 15:14, Kuzkin (roughing) 15:14, Stapleton (holding) 15:24

Third Period
5. Team Canada: Gilbert (Ratelle, D. Hull) 2:13
6. Soviet Union: Yakushev (Maltsev, Lutchenko) 5:15. Power-play goal
7. Team Canada: Henderson (Savard) 17:54
PENALTIES: Bergman (holding) 3:26, Gilbert (charging) 7:25, Bergman (major, roughing) 16:26, Mikhailov (major, roughing) 16:26.

[198]

SHOTS ON GOAL BY			
Team			
Canada	9	7	9 — 25
Soviet Union	6	13	12 — 31

SHOTS AT GOAL BY			
Team			
Canada	18	17	14 — 49
Soviet Union	14	26	24 — 64

Game #8, September 28, at Moscow.
Team Canada 6, Soviet Union 5

PLAYERS ON ICE

Team Canada: Bergman, Stapleton, Park, Ellis, P. Esposito,
Gilbert, D. Hull, Cournoyer, White, Ratelle, Henderson,
P. Mahovlich, Parise, Savard, Lapointe, F. Mahovlich,
Clarke.
Soviet Union: Gusev, Lutchenko, Kuzkin, Vasiliev, Tsygan-
kov, Blinov, Maltsev, Mishakov, Mikhailov, Yakushev,
Petrov, Kharlamov, Vikulov, Shadrin, Anisin, Liapkin,
Volchkov.

GOALTENDERS

Team Canada: Dryden, 60 minutes, 5 goals against.
Soviet Union: Tretiak, 60 minutes, 6 goals against.

SUMMARY

First Period
1. Soviet Union: Yakushev (Maltsev, Liapkin) 3:34.
   Power-play goal
2. Team Canada: P. Esposito (Park) 6:45. Power-play
   goal
3. Soviet Union: Lutchenko (Kharlamov) 13:10. Power-
   play goal
4. Team Canada: Park (Ratelle, D. Hull) 16:59
PENALTIES: White (holding) 2:25, P. Mahovlich (holding)
   3:01, Petrov (hooking) 3:44, Parise (minor, interference,
   10-minute misconduct, game misconduct) 4:10, Tsygankov (interference) 6:28, Ellis (interference) 9:27, Petrov
   (interference) 9:46, Cournoyer (interference) 12:51

Second Period
5. Soviet Union: Shadrin 00:21
6. Team Canada: White (Gilbert, Ratelle) 10:32
7. Soviet Union: Yakushev 11:43
8. Soviet Union: Vasiliev 16:44. Power-play goal
PENALTIES: Stapleton (cross-checking) 14:58, Kuzkin (elbowing) 18:06

Third Period
9. Team Canada: P. Esposito (P. Mahovlich) 2:27
10. Team Canada: Cournoyer (P. Esposito, Park) 12:56
11. Team Canada: Henderson (P. Esposito) 19:26
PENALTIES: Gilbert (major, fighting) 3:41, Mishakov (ma-

[200]

jor, fighting) 3:41, Vasiliev (tripping) 4:27, D. Hull
(high-sticking) 15:24, Petrov (elbowing) 15:24

SHOTS ON GOAL BY					SHOTS AT GOAL BY			
Team					Team			
Canada	14	8	14 — 36		Canada	25	20	25 — 70
Soviet					Soviet			
Union	12	10	5 — 27		Union	29	17	18 — 64

TEAM STATISTICS

Goals by	1st Period	2nd Period	3rd Period	Total
Soviet Union	9	12	11	32
Team Canada	9	10	12	31

Shots on Goal by				
Soviet Union	76	81	70	227
Team Canada	87	87	93	267

Shots at Goal by				
Soviet Union	188	170	159	517
Team Canada	163	162	156	481

TOTAL ADVANTAGES: Soviet Union 38 Team Canada 23

POWER-PLAY GOALS: Soviet Union 9 Team Canada 2

SHORTHANDED GOALS: Soviet Union 3 Team Canada 1

PENALTY MINUTES: Soviet Union 84 Team Canada 147

GOALTENDING RECORDS

Player	Games	Goals Against	Average
Esposito, Team Canada	4	13	3.25
Dryden, Team Canada	4	19	4.75
Tretiak, Soviet Union	8	31	3.87

Player	Games Played	Goals	Assists	Points	Penalty Minutes	Shots on Goal	Shots at Goal
Yakushev	8	7	4	11	4	21	48
Shadrin	8	3	5	8	0	15	28
Kharlamov	7	3	4	7	16	17	33
Petrov	8	3	4	7	10	19	40
Liapkin	6	1	5	6	0	15	34
Mikhailov	8	3	2	5	9	25	45
Maltsev	8	0	5	5	0	32	57
Anisin	7	1	3	4	2	9	30
Lutchenko	8	1	3	4	0	13	37
Zimin	2	2	1	3	0	5	8
Blinov	5	2	1	3	2	11	18
Vikulov	6	2	1	3	0	8	20
Vasiliev	6	1	2	3	6	5	17
Tsygankov	8	0	2	2	6	8	25
Lebedev	3	1	0	1	2	3	7
Bodunov	3	1	0	1	0	3	6
Gusev	6	1	0	1	2	5	14
Ragulin	6	0	1	1	4	4	14
Kuzkin	7	0	1	1	8	3	13
Martyniuk	1	0	0	0	0	3	4
Solodukhin	1	0	0	0	0	0	1
Starshinov	1	0	0	0	0	0	2
Shatalov	2	0	0	0	0	0	1
Volchkov	3	0	0	0	0	0	2
Paladiev	3	0	0	0	0	1	6
Mishakov	6	0	0	0	11	2	7
TOTALS	8	32	44	76	84 °	227	517

° Includes one bench minor to each team.

Own Team			Opposition			
For	(Power Play Goals)	Net	Agst	(Plus Power Play Goals)	Net	Overall Net
15	4	11	6	0	6	p 5
14	3	11	4	0	4	p 7
9	2	7	7	0	7	Even
9	4	5	11	0	11	m 6
11	3	8	6	1	5	p 3
8	4	4	8	0	8	m 4
8	3	5	11	0	11	m 6
7	0	7	4	0	4	p 3
16	8	8	10	1	9	m 1
4	0	4	3	0	3	p 1
4	1	3	5	0	5	m 2
6	2	4	13	1	12	m 8
6	1	5	4	0	4	p 1
9	2	7	13	1	12	m 5
1	0	1	3	0	3	m 2
2	0	2	3	0	3	m 1
3	0	3	4	0	4	m 1
5	0	5	8	1	7	m 2
6	2	4	9	0	9	m 5
0	0	0	0	0	0	Even
1	0	1	3	0	3	m 2
0	0	0	2	1	1	m 1
3	0	3	2	0	2	p 1
2	1	1	1	0	1	Even
5	0	5	3	0	3	p 2
0	0	0	9	2	7	m 7
32	9	23	31	2	29	m 6

Player	Games Played	Goals	Assists	Points	Penalty Minutes	Shots on Goal	Shots at Goal
P. Esposito	8	7	6	13	15	52	89
Henderson	8	7	3	10	4	28	38
Clarke	8	2	4	6	18	13	25
Cournoyer	8	3	2	5	2	27	46
Park	8	1	4	5	2	9	21
Hull	4	2	2	4	4	10	24
Parise	6	2	2	4	28	5	11
Gilbert	6	1	3	4	9	8	14
Ratelle	6	1	3	4	0	4	12
Bergman	8	0	3	3	13	6	9
Ellis	8	0	3	3	8	23	35
Perreault	2	1	1	2	0	4	11
Goldsworthy	3	1	1	2	4	3	6
F. Mahovlich	6	1	1	2	0	19	29
P. Mahovlich	7	1	1	2	4	12	22
White	7	1	1	2	8	6	13
Cashman	2	0	2	2	14	3	4
Savard	5	0	2	2	0	3	7
Mikita	2	0	1	1	0	1	3
Berenson	2	0	1	1	0	3	4
Lapointe	7	0	1	1	6	15	28
Redmond	1	0	0	0	0	1	4
Awrey	2	0	0	0	0	0	1
Hadfield	2	0	0	0	0	2	4
Seiling	3	0	0	0	0	2	4
Stapleton	7	0	0	0	6	8	17
TOTALS	8	31	46	77	147 *	267	481

* Includes one bench minor to each team.

ON ICE FOR GOALS BY

Own Team			Opposition			
For	(Power Play Goals)	Net	Agst	(Plus Power Play Goals)	Net	Overall Net
15	2	13	16	5	11	p 2
12	1	11	5	0	5	p 6
8	0	8	9	3	6	p 2
10	1	9	9	0	9	Even
15	2	13	14	5	9	p 4
6	0	6	2	0	2	p 4
6	0	6	5	0	5	p 1
5	0	5	4	0	4	p 1
4	0	4	6	0	6	m 2
12	0	12	12	5	7	p 5
10	1	9	9	3	6	p 3
2	0	2	0	0	0	p 2
2	0	2	2	0	2	Even
4	0	4	7	1	6	m 2
3	0	3	5	3	2	p 1
11	0	11	7	3	4	p 7
3	0	3	1	0	1	p 2
3	0	3	4	0	4	m 1
1	0	1	0	0	0	p 1
1	0	1	1	0	1	Even
9	2	7	10	0	10	m 3
0	0	0	1	0	1	m 1
0	0	0	2	0	2	m 2
0	0	0	3	0	3	m 3
2	0	2	8	0	8	m 6
10	0	10	7	3	4	p 6
31	2	29	32	9	23	p 6

TEAM CANADA VS. SWEDEN

Game #1, September 16, at Stockholm.
Team Canada 4, Sweden 1

PLAYERS ON ICE

Team Canada: Bergman, Stapleton, Park, Ellis, P. Esposito, Gilbert, Hadfield, Cashman, White, Ratelle, Henderson, P. Mahovlich, Parise, Redmond, Clarke, Dionne, Guevremont, Glennie.

Sweden (Tre Kronor): Carlsson, Ostling, Salming, T. Abrahamsson, Sjoberg, Johansson, Wickberg, Lundstrom, Sterner, Soderstom, Larbraton, Nilsson, Ahlberg, Palmquist, Hammarstrom, Hedberg, Yderstrom, Milton.

GOALTENDERS

Team Canada: T. Esposito, 60 minutes, 1 goal against.
Sweden: C. Abrahamsson, 60 minutes, 4 goals against.

SUMMARY

First Period
1. Team Canada: Henderson (Ellis) 1:45
PENALTIES: Cashman (hooking) 3:22, Hadfield (slashing) 14:36

Second Period
2. Team Canada: Clarke (Ellis, Bergman) 1:14
3. Sweden: Sterner (Sjoberg, Salming) 3:51. Power-play goal
PENALTIES: P. Esposito (cross-checking minor, charging minor, 10-minute misconduct) 2:26, Bergman (tripping) 2:53, T. Abrahamsson (interference) 4:35, Salming (tripping) 8:00, Clarke (elbowing) 11:33, P. Mahovlich (slashing) 11:39, Sterner (tripping) 19:48

Third Period
4. Team Canada: Park (P. Esposito, Cashman) 9:15
5. Team Canada: Cashman (P. Esposito, Parise) 16:34
PENALTIES: Cashman (roughing) 6:45, Carlsson (interference) 9:26

SHOTS ON GOAL BY

Team Canada	11	11	12 — 34
Sweden	10	7	7 — 24

Game #2, September 17, at Stockholm.
Team Canada 4, Sweden 4

PLAYERS ON ICE

Team Canada: Stapleton, Park, P. Esposito, Gilbert, Goldsworthy, D. Hull, Hadfield, Cournoyer, Cashman, Berenson, Seiling, Ratelle, Mikita, Parise, Awrey, Tallon, Perreault, Martin, Guevremont.

Sweden (Tre Kronor): Carlsson, Ostling, Salming, T. Abrahamsson, Sjoberg, Sundquist, Johansson, Wickberg, Lundstrom, Sterner, Nilsson, Ahlberg, Lindh, Palmquist, Hammarstrom, Hedberg, Yderstrom, Hansson.

GOALTENDERS

Team Canada: Johnston, 60 minutes, 4 goals against.
Sweden: Larsson, 60 minutes, 4 goals against.

SUMMARY

First Period

1. Team Canada: Hadfield (Gilbert, Stapleton) 10:30
PENALTIES: Parise (holding) 13:10, Goldsworthy (cross-checking minor, spearing minor, 10-minute misconduct) 16:26.

Second Period

2. Sweden: Nilsson (Sjoberg) 1:12
3. Team Canada: Awrey 9:15
PENALTIES: Tallon (slashing) 5:03, Salming (tripping) 12:44

Third Period

4. Sweden: Lundstrom (Johansson) 3:16
5. Team Canada: Martin (Perreault, Cournoyer) 3:32
6. Sweden: Hansson (Hedberg) 7:09. Power-play goal
7. Sweden: Hammarstrom 11:16. Power-play goal
8. Team Canada, P. Esposito (Tallon) 19:13. Shorthanded goal
PENALTIES: P. Esposito (hooking) 6:27, Ratelle (tripping) 9:15, Parise (hooking) 11:02, Hadfield (major, high-sticking) 14:31, Tallon (roughing) 16:18, Sterner (roughing) 16:18

SHOTS ON GOAL BY

Team Canada	7	9	10 — 26
Sweden	10	11	17 — 38

[207]

TEAM CANADA VS. CZECHOSLOVAKIA

September 29, at Prague.
Team Canada 3, Czechoslovakia 3

Team Canada: Park, P. Esposito, Goldsworthy, D. Hull, Cournoyer, Cashman, Seiling, P. Mahovlich, Mikita, Parise, Savard, Redmond, Awrey, F. Mahovlich, Clarke, Tallon, Dionne, Glennie.

Czechoslovakia: Horesovsky, Machac, Jaroslav Holik, Pospisil, Kochta, Klapac, Martinec, Farda, Stastny, Nedomansky, Palecek, Bubla, Kuzela, Bednar, Jiri Holik, Hlinka, Brunclik, Emerman.

GOALTENDERS

Team Canada: Dryden, 60 minutes, 3 goals against.
Czechoslovakia: Holecek, 60 minutes, 3 goals against.

SUMMARY

First Period

1. Team Canada: Savard (Park) 8:19. Power-play goal
2. Team Canada: P. Mahovlich (Tallon) 13:55
PENALTIES: Awrey (high-sticking) 7:12, Stastny (high-sticking) 7:12, Bubla (interference) 8:09, Goldsworthy (hooking) 9:26

Second Period

3. Czechoslovakia: Stastny (Bubla) 9:02
4. Czechoslovakia: Stastny 15:24. Power-play goal
PENALTIES: D. Hull (tripping) 3:58, Redmond (charging) 9:26, Tallon (high-sticking) 13:43, Mikita (cross-checking) 16:57, Jaroslav Holik (elbowing) 16:57, Clarke (major, high-sticking) 20:00, Pospisil (elbowing) 20:00.

Third Period

5. Czechoslovakia: Kochta (Holecek) 2:28. Power-play goal
6. Team Canada: Savard (Clarke, Park) 19:56
PENALTY: Hlinka (hooking) 4:42.

SHOTS ON GOAL BY			
Team Canada	13	3	8 — 24
Czechoslovakia	12	12	9 — 33

Picture Credits

THE INTERSUBJECTIVITY OF THE MYSTIC
A Study of Teresa of Avila's
Interior Castle

American Academy of Religion Academy Series

edited by
Susan Thistlethwaite

Number 83
THE INTERSUBJECTIVITY OF THE MYSTIC
A Study of Teresa of Avila's
Interior Castle

by
Mary Frohlich